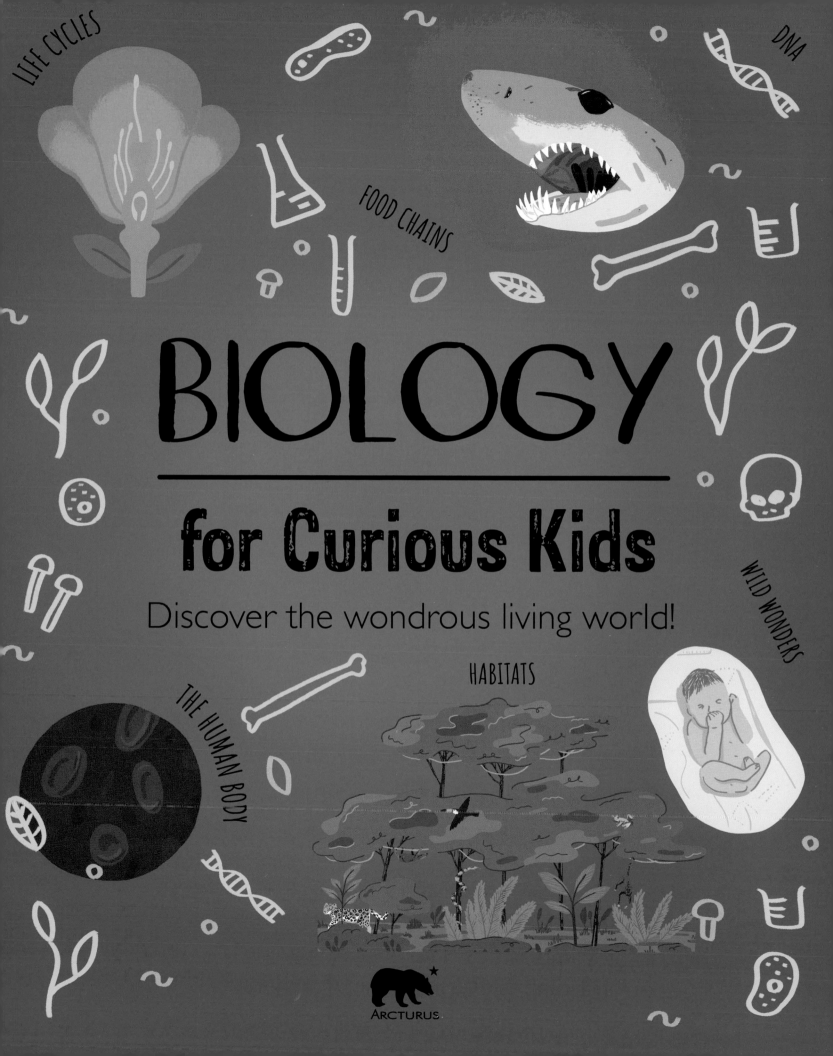

LIFE CYCLES

DNA

FOOD CHAINS

BIOLOGY
for Curious Kids
Discover the wondrous living world!

WILD WONDERS

HABITATS

THE HUMAN BODY

ARCTURUS

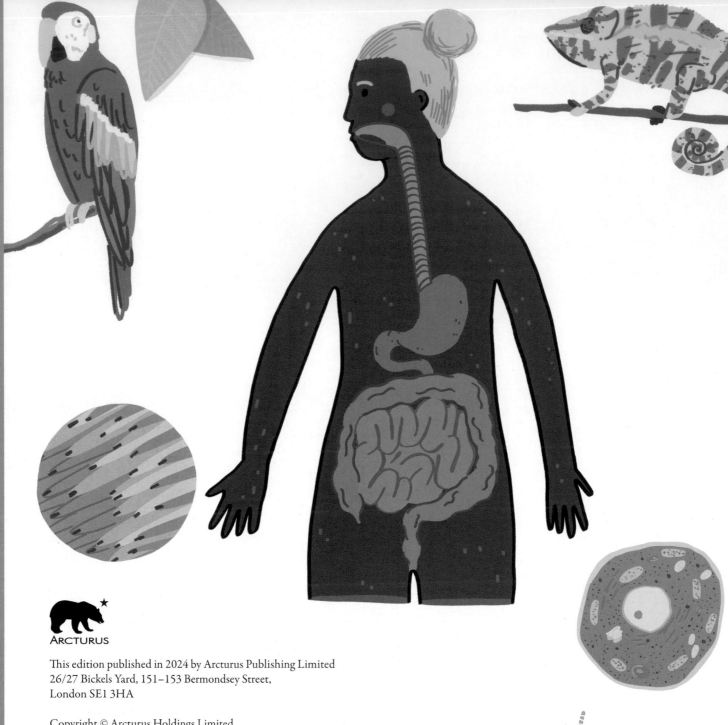

This edition published in 2024 by Arcturus Publishing Limited
26/27 Bickels Yard, 151–153 Bermondsey Street,
London SE1 3HA

Author: Laura Baker
Illustrator: Alex Foster
Consultant: Anne Rooney
Designer: Jeanette Ryall
Packaged by Cloud King Creative

ISBN: 978-1-3988-0259-9
CH008269US
Supplier 29, Date 0524, PI 00006727

Printed in China

What is STEM?

STEM is a world-wide initiative that aims to cultivate an interest in
Science, Technology, Engineering, and Mathematics, in an effort to
promote these disciplines to as wide a variety of students as possible.

CONTENTS

WELCOME TO THE WORLD OF BIOLOGY

Biology is the study of all **living organisms**, big or small, old or new, animal or plant, and more. Studying biology can tell us about what our planet used to look like, how life began, and where it might go next.

Biology is broken down into many different areas of study. Some people study plants and their importance to humans and other living things. Others dive into the animal kingdom and wonder at the millions of **species** there are to discover. Others look at the human body, from bones to brains to blood! And some scientists like to go microscopic, studying the tiniest organisms that we know.

The people who study biology are called **biologists**. Whatever their field, they all have one major thing in common: they are interested in finding answers to questions about life.

Become a biologist yourself as you journey through these pages and uncover some of the mysteries of our incredible living world.

WHAT IS LIFE?

Before we can begin the study of life, we need to know what "life" is. Is it something that can think? Breathe? Grow? What makes a living, growing blade of grass different from a non-living, growing flame? What makes people different from robots? And where did it all begin?

Key features

Scientists agree that there are some key, common features that must exist for something to be alive:

It moves substances, such as food, around its body.

It reacts to its environment.

It needs and uses energy.

It usually grows and may change as it does so.

It exchanges gases, such as oxygen, with its environment.

It can reproduce, by having babies or making copies of itself.

So, although a fire grows, it doesn't move food around its body. And while a robot can react to its environment, it cannot reproduce.

UNANSWERED QUESTIONS

New species (or groups of similar living things) continue to be discovered, and scientific developments are always being made. This begs the question: If there are things we don't know, how can we be sure about what we do? As we build robots that can copy themselves, might we need to redefine what life is? What about life beyond planet Earth? Scientific discoveries can sometimes lead to more questions than answers—but that's the beauty of studying biology.

PHILOSOPHY AND SCIENCE

The famous Greek philosopher Aristotle was born in Greece around 384 BCE. He looked at the question of life **philosophically**, questioning what defined life and knowledge. He concluded that life was anything that could grow and reproduce. Since Aristotle's time, scientists have narrowed down this definition further, but many of his ideas remain.

In fact, Aristotle is often thought of as an early scientist. Unlike other philosophers, he didn't just do his work in his mind—he was hands-on, studying organisms and making observations. He was one of the first to divide animals into smaller classifications, making him not only one of the founders of philosophy, but also of biology.

CHAPTER 1

MICROBIOLOGY: THE BUILDING BLOCKS OF LIFE

Whether it's a blue whale, the largest animal on Earth, or the tiniest of **bacteria,** each living **organism** is made up of **cells**. Some creatures are complete with just a single cell, while others are made of millions or more. The human body is formed of trillions of cells!

Microbiology is the study of **microorganisms**—the living things so small that you need a microscope to see them. In this chapter we'll look at the chemical building blocks of life and peer through the microscope to see cells at work.

BUILDING LIFE

Biology and chemistry collide when we begin to talk about the building blocks of life. From chemistry we know that there are over a hundred natural **elements** that make up everything in the universe. A small selection of these elements is what allows life to exist on Earth. Without them, life simply could not be.

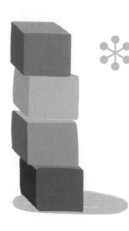

IN YOUR ELEMENT

BREAK IT DOWN

An element is something that cannot be broken down into a simpler substance. Some are metallic, such as gold and silver. Some are gas at Earth's usual surface temperatures, while others are solid or liquid. Each element is made of a different type of atom. Everything on the planet is made up of one or more elements.

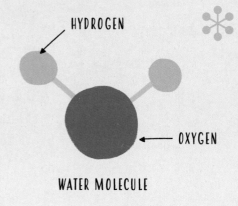

HYDROGEN

OXYGEN

WATER MOLECULE

OXYGEN AND HYDROGEN

Hydrogen is the most abundant element in the universe, meaning there is more of it than any other element. It is also the lightest. Hydrogen atoms often bond with oxygen atoms to create water molecules. A molecule is a group of atoms that are bonded together. Separately, oxygen also exists as the part of the air that many organisms need to breathe to survive.

NITROGEN

Nitrogen makes up nearly 80% of Earth's atmosphere. It is also found within organisms as a part of large molecules called proteins, along with other elements such as oxygen, hydrogen, and carbon. Every cell in your body contains proteins.

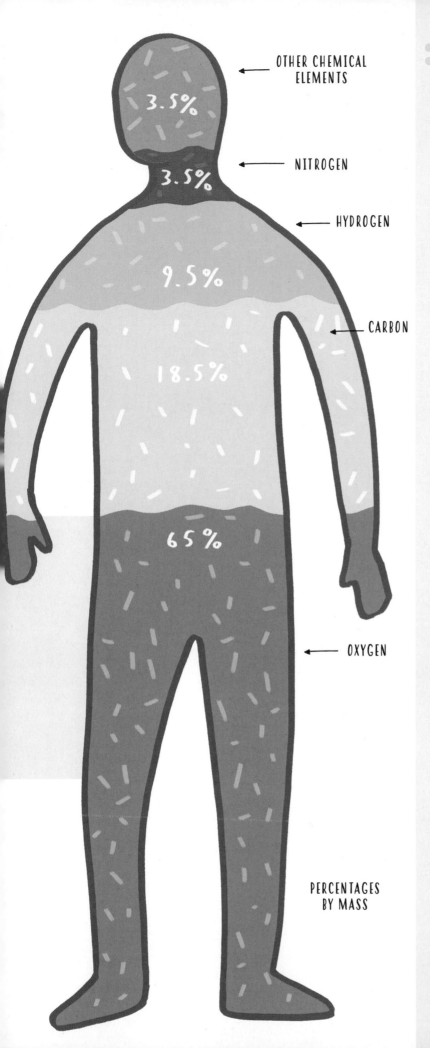

OTHER CHEMICAL ELEMENTS

3.5%

NITROGEN

3.5%

HYDROGEN

9.5%

CARBON

18.5%

65%

OXYGEN

PERCENTAGES BY MASS

CARBON

Carbon is the most important element in creating and sustaining all life on Earth. It is especially good at bonding in different ways with other elements, forming **organic compounds**. Variations of carbon-based compounds are found in millions of living things. These are grouped into four main types.

1. Carbohydrates: These molecules are formed of carbon, hydrogen, and oxygen. They include sugars and starches and provide energy to living cells.

2. Lipids: These are greasy or waxy substances such as fats and oils. They can store energy for an organism and form cell membranes (the outer layer).

3. Proteins: These are large and important molecules that play a vital part in life. They build cells, speed up chemical reactions (changes in molecules), and carry messages and materials through organisms.

4. Nucleic acids: These carry instructions to make proteins as well as information on cell functions and reproduction. For example, nearly every cell in the human body holds **DNA** (deoxyribonucleic acid), which is like a coded instruction manual for reproducing and taking care of our cells.

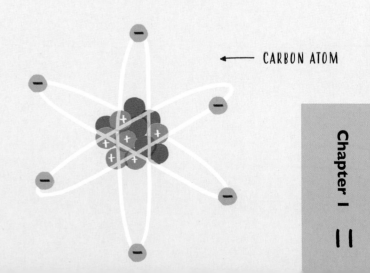

CARBON ATOM

Chapter 1

11

CODING LIFE

Every living thing carries a code that determines how the organism will look and function. These instructions are held on strands of DNA, or **deoxyribonucleic acid**, found in nearly all living cells. DNA is what makes you uniquely **you**.

LADDER OF LIFE

DNA is a long, stringy **molecule** (group of atoms bonded together) made of two strands with links between them. These are twisted into a spiral ladder structure, called a **double helix**. The ladder has rungs made of four chemical bases—adenine, cytosine, thymine, and guanine.

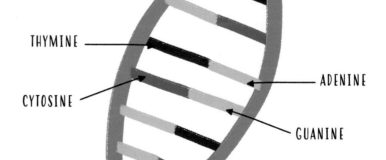

THYMINE

CYTOSINE

ADENINE

GUANINE

The bases always appear in pairs. This is an extremely clever feature of DNA. It means that when a cell needs to reproduce, for example to help the organism grow or heal, the DNA splits itself down the middle of the ladder to create two new strands. These are easily completed by matching pairs to create exact copies of the original chain.

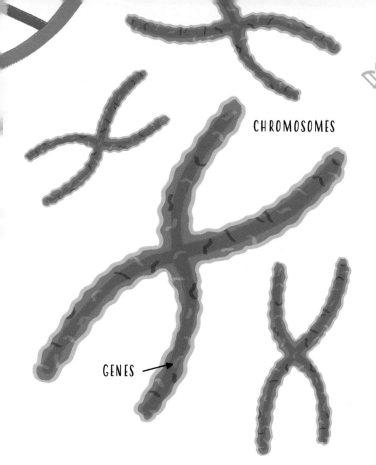

CHROMOSOMES

GENES →

DEEP IN DNA

DNA holds the secret recipe for an individual organism. Within a molecule of DNA are short sections called **genes**. Each gene carries a different piece of information. The pieces of information control characteristics such as eye shade, height, and nose shape.

Genes are held within **chromosomes**. These are coiled strands of DNA found within a cell's **nucleus.** Humans have 46 chromosomes holding over 20,000 genes across them. We inherit half our chromosomes from each parent (23 from each). This is how you can have some of your father's features and some of your mother's. Other organisms have different numbers of chromosomes. Fruit flies, for example, have just eight, while a red king crab has 208!

DETECTIVE DNA

Since each person's DNA is unique (unless you are an identical twin), it can be used as a way to identify us. This makes DNA the perfect tool for solving a crime. People called **forensic scientists**—experts who use science in criminal investigations—gather DNA from a crime scene in cells such as hair or saliva. They analyze the cells to create a **DNA profile.** This is a picture of part of the suspect's DNA. They can then use this to try to find a DNA match, and the culprit.

OUT OF CURIOSITY

We share about half of our genes with a banana! That's because most genes just control how an organism works: how it carries out chemical reactions to grow and use energy. All organisms do that in much the same way because they have all evolved from the simple single-celled organisms that appeared billions of years ago.

Chapter 1

13

BACK TO BASICS

Cells are only small, but they play a big part in life. Every living thing—plant, animal, or other—is made of cells. Most are too tiny to see without a microscope. But all have their own important role. There are millions of different types of cells, giving us the basic units of life.

INSIDE A CELL

Within a cell are various structures that help perform that cell's particular function. Every animal cell has several main elements. The nucleus holds DNA and controls what goes on. The **cell membrane** surrounds the cell and allows **nutrients** to pass in and out. The **cytoplasm** is a jelly-like substance where chemical reactions happen, changing one molecule to another. **Mitochondria** give life to the cell, releasing energy from nutrients through chemical reactions.

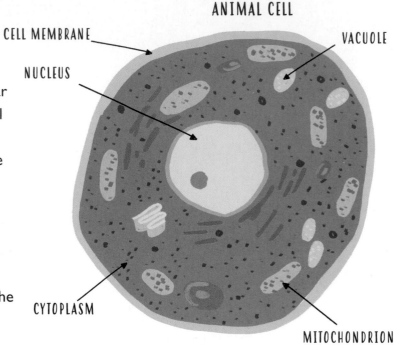

ANIMAL CELL

CELL MEMBRANE
NUCLEUS
VACUOLE
CYTOPLASM
MITOCHONDRION

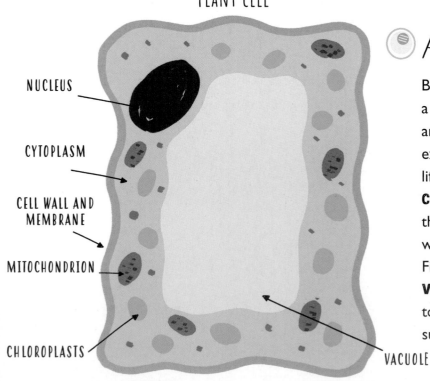

PLANT CELL

NUCLEUS
CYTOPLASM
CELL WALL AND MEMBRANE
MITOCHONDRION
CHLOROPLASTS
VACUOLE

ANIMAL OR PLANT

Both animal and plant cells have a nucleus, cell membrane, cytoplasm, and mitochondria. A plant cell has some extra features, too, to maintain its unique life. Outside the cell membrane is a stiff **cell wall** to support the cell. Within the cytoplasm are green **chloroplasts**, which create nutrients for the plant. Finally, both plant and animal cells have **vacuoles**: spaces that store material to help control conditions in the cell, such as how floppy or firm it is.

MAKING MORE CELLS

Living organisms grow, heal, and reproduce by making new cells. There are two main ways that a cell can replicate (copy) itself.

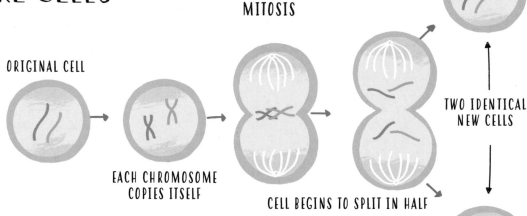

MITOSIS

ORIGINAL CELL

EACH CHROMOSOME COPIES ITSELF

CELL BEGINS TO SPLIT IN HALF

TWO IDENTICAL NEW CELLS

1 In **mitosis**, a cell divides and creates two identical copies. To do so, each **chromosome** makes a copy of itself so that there are two full sets of chromosomes. These are then split evenly, with one set moving to each end of the original cell as it begins to divide into two. This process is carried out so accurately that each new cell carries the same genetic make-up as the first. These identical cells are the means by which the organism grows and heals.

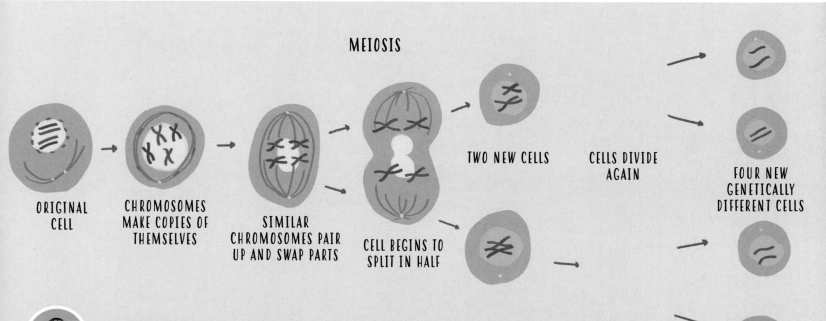

MEIOSIS

ORIGINAL CELL

CHROMOSOMES MAKE COPIES OF THEMSELVES

SIMILAR CHROMOSOMES PAIR UP AND SWAP PARTS

CELL BEGINS TO SPLIT IN HALF

TWO NEW CELLS

CELLS DIVIDE AGAIN

FOUR NEW GENETICALLY DIFFERENT CELLS

2 **Meiosis** is used for reproduction and creating brand-new life. A cell divides **twice** to create four cells that contain **half** the genetic information of the first. In contrast to mitosis, similar chromosomes pair up and swap chunks between them. When the cell splits in half, each new cell has a different mixture of genes. The two new cells then divide again, so that there are now four cells genetically different from the original and each with half the number of chromosomes. When one of these cells from each parent comes together to make a baby, they each bring half the chromosomes the baby needs.

Chapter 1

15

CELL FACTORY

Each cell inside your body—and inside every living organism—is buzzing with activity. Some cells carry oxygen, some help you think, some store energy, and some protect you. Inside your body are trillions of little factories working hard to keep you alive.

NUCLEUS

If the cell is a factory, the **nucleus** is the control and command desk, or the boss. It tells the cell how to grow, replicate, and work. Inside the nucleus are the **chromosomes** that hold the DNA. They keep the blueprints to show how the factory's products should look.

RIBOSOMES

Ribosomes are busy workers on the factory floor. They make proteins, reading the code in the DNA to find out how to make each one. Proteins control all functions in the body.

WORKING IN A PLANT CELL

NUCLEUS

CHROMOSOMES

CELL MEMBRANE

RIBOSOMES

CHLOROPLASTS

MITOCHONDRIA

CELL MEMBRANE

The **cell membrane** is the shipping and receiving department. It allows useful materials to enter the cell and sends out products and waste that the cell has made.

ENERGY

Both the **mitochondria** and **chloroplasts** (in a plant) are the factory's power source. Between them, they manage at a cellular level the energy the organism needs.

CELL SPECIALTIES

One organism can be made of many different types of cells. These work together to make the organism and keep it working.

For example, the human body has about 200 different types of cells that perform different functions. Each has a different shape and inner structure to perform its function perfectly.

MICRO POWER!

NERVE CELLS

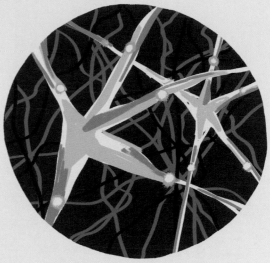

Nerve cells transmit nerve signals between the brain and different parts of the body and within the brain.

RED BLOOD CELLS

Red blood cells carry oxygen through the body.

SKIN CELLS

Skin cells protect everything inside the body.

FAT CELLS

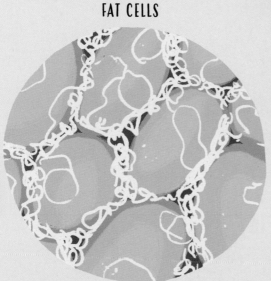

Fat cells store energy as fat.

MUSCLE CELLS

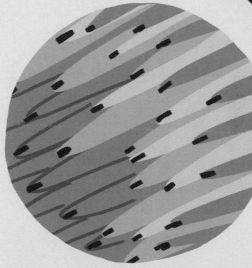

Muscle cells enable your body to move.

GOING MICROSCOPIC

At the microscopic level, a whole other world exists. Tiny cells invisible to the naked eye are busy with their own lives. These are microorganisms, or microbes. Some help us, some can be harmful—and some have no effect on us at all!

MICROORGANISMS

A microorganism is exactly that: an organism that is "micro," or microscopic. They can only be seen using a **microscope**. **Viruses** are too small to be seen with a normal microscope.

VIRUSES

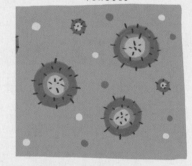

TARDIGRADE

Some microorganisms have only one cell. Others are tiny plants and animals, such as tardigrades, with many cells.

ARCHAEA

OUT OF CURIOSITY

When the microscope was invented in the early 17th century, people discovered the astonishing world of microorganisms. Since then, microscopes have been getting more and more powerful. Today, we can magnify things up to 500,000 times their size!

SINGLE CELLS

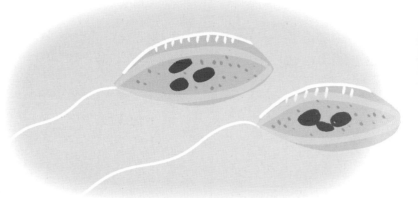

Most microorganisms are just one cell. These are called **single-celled organisms**. These were the very first life forms on planet Earth, around 4 billion years ago, emerging in the oceans. These earliest cells were **prokaryotic** cells, which are simpler than plant and animal cells, known as **eukaryotes**. In a **prokaryote**, DNA floats freely, rather than in a nucleus. Today's **bacteria** and **archaea** (see page 25) are prokaryotes, while all other living things are made of eukaryotic cells.

Protozoa are single-celled eukaryotes. Some have tails, hair, or even foot-like pseudopods. They feed on bacteria, algae, and micro-fungi.

Fungi are eukaryotes that can be single-celled or many-celled. They feed on animal and plant matter and are important in decomposing natural waste. Yeast is a fungus that turns sugar into carbon dioxide gas, so it is used to make bread fluffy. Some fungi cause diseases, but others are used in medicines.

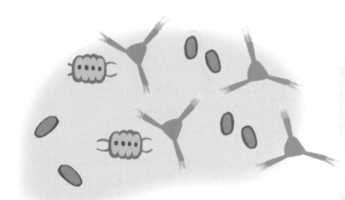

Plankton are tiny living things that drift and float in oceans and fresh water, where they are eaten by fish and other living things. Plankton can be bacteria, plant-like algae, protozoa—or even little animals and plants.

Helpful microbes

We often hear bad things about bacteria, fungi, and other tiny organisms, but some can be helpful to humans. For example, bacteria called *Rhizobium* are found in soil and provide nutrients to plants. In the food industry, bacteria such as *Lactobacillus* can change milk into cheese and yogurt.

THE GOOD, BAD, AND UGLY

Bacteria and **viruses** are well known for making us sick, but although this is true, many bacteria don't deserve this reputation. Many help plants and animals with important survival mechanisms.

BACTERIA

A **bacterium** is a single-celled organism. Bacteria cells have a cell wall, but no nucleus. Instead, DNA floats in the cytoplasm. There are millions of different types of bacteria, each with its own shape and structure. Some have tails to move around. Some have outer slime to protect themselves.

DIGESTIVE SYSTEM

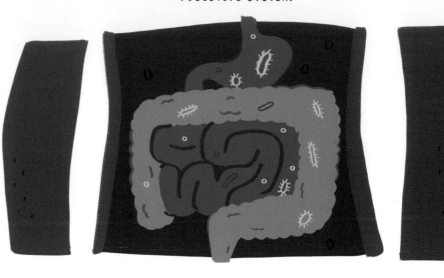

BAD BACTERIA

Some bacteria can make people and animals ill. They can cause **diseases** such as food poisoning or meningitis. Once inside the body, the bacteria cells reproduce quickly. The body tries to eject or kill these intruders with strategies such as sneezing, fever, and vomiting.

There are medicines that can kill bacteria. In 1928, scientist Sir Alexander Fleming discovered **penicillin**, a substance produced by a fungus that works as a medicine called an **antibiotic**. Antibiotics attack the bacteria that cause infections in humans and animals and are now used all over the world to save lives.

GOOD BACTERIA

There are billions of bacteria cells within your body that help to keep you healthy. Some live on the skin, others in the nose, and others even in the mouth. In the digestive system alone, millions of bacteria help break down and digest food. Many of the good bacteria in your body work to fight off bad bacteria!

VIRUSES

Unfortunately, viruses are not as helpful as good bacteria. These sneaky things make animals, plants, and other living things sick. In humans, they cause colds, flus, measles, and other diseases, such as COVID-19. Viruses are not made of cells: their DNA is wrapped simply in a **protein** coat. Scientists do not agree on whether we can call them "living things" or not. Viruses can only reproduce by entering the cell of a living thing, then using the machinery of the cell to make copies of themselves.

COLD OR FLU VIRUS

MEASLES VIRUS

The body's **immune system** works hard to fight viruses once they are inside. Viruses can't be treated by antibiotics, so the best thing to do is to avoid them getting in your body in the first place by washing your hands and wearing a mask when appropriate.

OUT OF CURIOSITY

Some deep-sea fish have bacteria that can produce light to lure in prey in the deep dark sea.

MICRO LIFE

Even though we can't see them, microorganisms are going about their own lives—even in strange and surprising environments, from carpets to the deep ocean. Some of the most amazing microorganisms are not bacteria or fungi, but teeny-tiny animals.

MICRO BEAR

You'd never know it but minuscule **tardigrades**, or water bears, are walking and swimming around in water and mud. They have eight legs, tiny claws, and can live in such extreme conditions that they can survive in space!

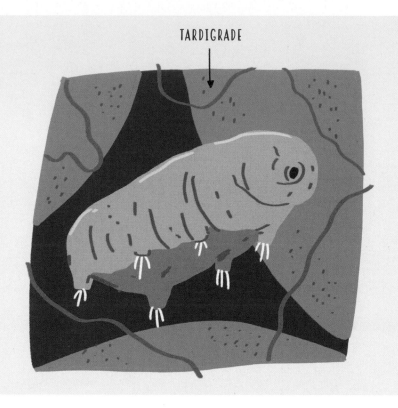

TARDIGRADE

MITES

Mites are teeny-tiny arachnids (like spiders), with eight legs. Many need a plant or animal **host** to feed on. Dust mites don't attach to humans but instead find dead skin cells around the house and like to bury themselves in carpets and rugs. They can make you sneeze or itch.

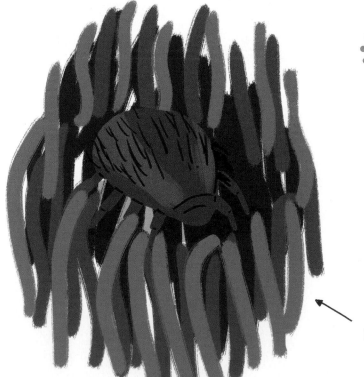

DUST MITE

BACK TO LIFE

A mysterious tiny animal called the **bdelloid** lives in puddles, moisture in soil, and other fresh water. The astonishing thing is that if the water—their home and source of food—disappears, they can dry up and survive for years. When water returns, they rehydrate and carry on!

 # EXTREME HEAT

Deep at the bottom of the sea, the archaeon (see page 25) *Geogemma barossii* survives in extreme heat that would kill almost any other living organism. This microbe thrives in conditions as hot as 121°C (250°F), feeding on minerals around hydrothermal vents that blast out hot water into the ocean.

 # STRENGTH IN NUMBERS

Coral polyps are animals no bigger than a pencil tip, but grouped together they can build coral reefs thousands of miles long. Reefs are made of the outer skeletons of groups of coral polyps, each skeleton growing on and beside countless others. Coral polyps are related to jellyfish—which can range in size from about 1 cm (0.4 in) to 36 m (118 ft) long!

 # BIG...

The largest single-celled organism can actually be seen by the naked eye. It is a seaweed, a plant-like alga called *Caulerpa taxifolia*. It can grow to 30 cm (12 in) long—nearly as tall as a bowling pin.

 # ...SMALL

In contrast, the smallest known microorganisms are bacteria such as *Mycoplasma*. These are so small that 200 of them could fit on the tip of a single strand of your hair. These cells are stripped back to the very basics, with no cell wall at all.

CORAL POLYPS

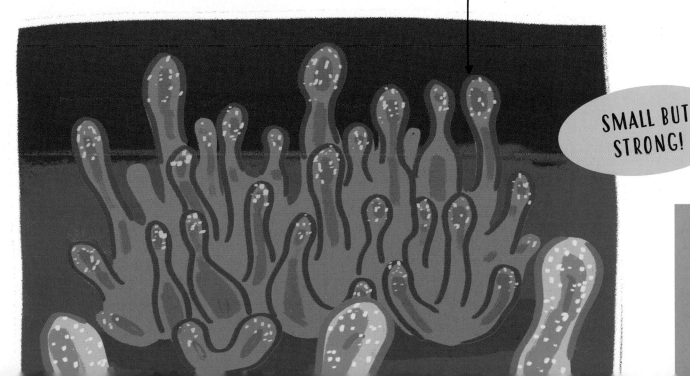

SMALL BUT STRONG!

Chapter 1

23

KINGDOMS OF LIFE

Every creature, big or small, is **classified** into a kingdom of life. These group life forms by features they share. In the 1700s, organisms were divided into two categories—plant or animal. Now, with more advanced science and super-strong microscopes that can detect the tiniest speck, many scientists agree on **six kingdoms** of life.

 ## ANIMALS

This kingdom includes millions of species (groups of similar-looking organisms that can reproduce together). Animals range from simple organisms such as sea sponges, to huge whales and clever creatures such as humans. The life forms in this kingdom cannot produce their own food, so they eat other organisms.

 ## PLANTS

From tiny floating duckweed to towering trees, plants can be found all over the world—even in the ocean! These multi-celled organisms produce their own food, by using the energy of sunlight and chemicals around them. This kingdom is crucial to supporting most life on Earth.

 ## FUNGI

The fungus kingdom includes both single and multiple-celled organisms. These life forms were thought to be plants in the past, but scientists now know they are very different. Unlike plants, fungi do not produce their own food. Instead, they absorb (or soak up) nutrients from matter such as dead plants and animals.

BACTERIA

This group of prokaryotes (see page 19) is found all over the world, in all environments and nearly all conditions, including inside plants and animals. Bacteria get their energy from sunlight or by breaking down chemicals or dead organisms. Some can move using hair-like pilli or tail-like flagella.

ARCHAEA

These prokaryotes look like bacteria but many thrive in hostile conditions, such as volcanic vents in the ocean, hot springs, or highly salty seas. They were only recently discovered but are in fact thought to be among the oldest types of living organisms on Earth.

PROTISTS

In this kingdom are eukaryotic (see page 19) single-celled and many-celled organisms. The kingdom includes algae, protozoa, slime molds—and anything else that doesn't fit into the other categories! Protists can produce their own food or feed on other organisms.

CHAPTER 2

BOTANY: THE WORLD OF PLANTS

Plants cover much of our planet's surface, from blades of grass to floating lily pads to towering trees. They provide us with food, materials, and even oxygen to breathe. There are hundreds of thousands of different species of plants—and **botanists** study all of them!

Botany is the study of plants and plant life. This includes the characteristics of plants, what plants need to survive and thrive, where you can find them across Planet Earth, and how plants can help us and our world. Let your curiosity blossom and your plant knowledge bloom as you travel through this botanical chapter.

Plants provide us with beautiful scenery, shelter, materials, and food to eat. They transform the air we breathe. If plants weren't on Earth, people and other animals wouldn't be either.

CIRCLE OF LIFE

Plants absorb a gas called **carbon dioxide** from the air and give off **oxygen** in return. Humans need that oxygen to breathe, and if there was too much carbon dioxide in the air, we couldn't survive. In fact, people and other animals breathe out carbon dioxide— which plants then absorb! It's one of those extraordinary cycles that keep life going.

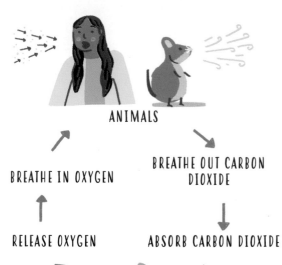

ANIMALS

BREATHE IN OXYGEN

BREATHE OUT CARBON DIOXIDE

RELEASE OXYGEN

ABSORB CARBON DIOXIDE

PLANTS

THANK YOU, PLANTS

FOOD AND SHELTER

Not only do plants give us oxygen, but they also give us food. They are at the bottom of most food chains, as many animals eat plants to survive. On top of that, plants provide homes and shelter for wildlife, from woodland birds in tall trees to tiny beetles in fallen leaves.

PHOTOSYNTHESIS

Photosynthesis is a process that happens inside green plants to produce food for them to survive. It is all about harnessing the power of the sun and storing it as **energy** that can be used by the plant.

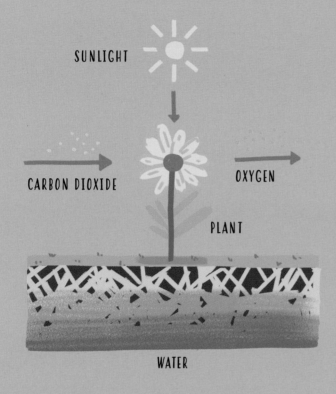

SUNLIGHT

CARBON DIOXIDE

OXYGEN

PLANT

WATER

1. The sun shines down on the plant. A green substance called chlorophyll in a plant's leaves absorbs the sun's energy.

2. A plant's roots soak up water from the ground, while a plant's leaves absorb carbon dioxide from the air.

3. Using energy from the sunlight, the plant combines the carbon dioxide and water to make a sugar called glucose.

4. A plant uses the glucose for energy. Oxygen is created in the process and is released into the air.

BABY PLANTS

Plants are **living things**, and just like animals, they have to reproduce. Different plants reproduce in different ways. Many plants produce **seeds**, which are tiny "baby" plants wrapped in a protective case, along with a food store. Seeds may form inside flowers (see page 31), inside cones (see page 34), or in fruit. Other plants, such as ferns, reproduce by releasing **spores**, which are simpler than seeds. If the seeds or spores land in the right spot and get the right amount of water and sunshine, they will grow into new plants, and the cycle begins again.

Chapter 2

29

PARTS OF A WHOLE

Whether a plant is big or small, flowering or not, most plants have the same basic parts. These parts work together to help the plant function perfectly—carrying out photosynthesis and reproducing.

LEAVES

Photosynthesis happens in the leaves of plants. They have tiny holes that are used for gas exchange, taking in carbon dioxide and releasing oxygen, and for letting water out.

STEM

The stem helps **support** the plant, usually by keeping it standing upright. It carries water and nutrients from the roots toward leaves and flowers. A tree's **trunk** is a hard, woody stem, made of tough cellulose and lignin.

ROOTS

A plant's roots hold it in place. Usually, roots reach into the ground, but some wrap around other plants or even reach into the air. Roots take in water and minerals to supply the plant with important **nutrients**.

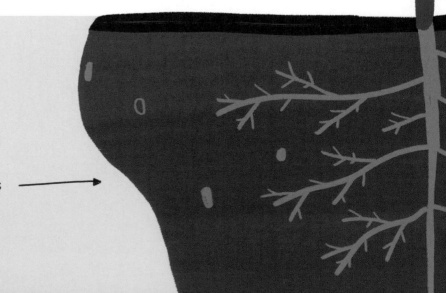

FLOWERS

Not all plants grow flowers, but the ones that do rely on them to **reproduce**. Flowers are often bright or smelly to attract bees, butterflies, and other animals that carry pollen to the plant so it can make seeds (see page 38). Although most flowers smell nice, some smell like rotting flesh to attract flies!

TO EACH ITS OWN

Each plant is adapted to its environment, with different features to help it survive. Some plants, such as potatoes and carrots, store food in swollen **underground** stems or roots. This helps them survive winter.

Some plants, such as moss, don't have roots or stems. These are called **non-vascular** plants. They live in damp places so they can absorb moisture. These simple plants often grow low to the ground.

LEAVE IT TO THE LEAF

The leaf is where the magic happens, making food for the plant to survive. Just like plants themselves, leaves are many different shapes and sizes. However, most leaves share the same basic features.

The leaf's **veins** transport water and nutrients from the stem to different parts of the leaf. Once photosynthesis has taken place, the veins also transport the **glucose** that was created to the rest of the plant for energy.

The **petiole** connects the leaf to the plant's stem. It connects with the **midrib**, which provides support to the leaf, helping it to stand strong whatever the weather.

On the underside of the leaf are tiny **stomata**: little holes that allow carbon dioxide to go in and oxygen to flow out.

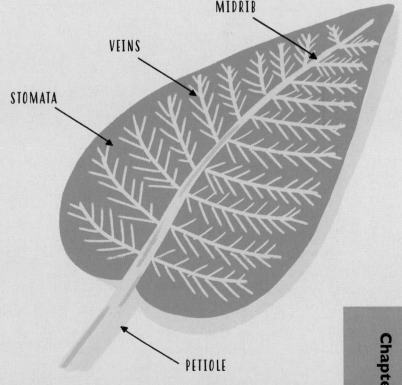

MIDRIB

VEINS

STOMATA

PETIOLE

SURVIVING AND THRIVING

Just like us, a plant needs certain things to thrive in the world. It requires food, drink, and a few other special ingredients for survival on Planet Earth.

SUNLIGHT

OUT OF CURIOSITY

While plants can't speak, some can in fact communicate with each other! They release chemicals to warn other plants if insects are attacking.

HAPPY, HEALTHY GREENS

How do you know if a plant is healthy? It can't smile or talk, but it does have other ways of telling us. Most plants show their strength by standing upright with bright green leaves open. If a plant starts to wilt, it may not be getting everything it needs. A healthy plant may turn itself toward the sun to take in more light, and its roots branch out in search of water and nutrients.

LIGHT AND WARMTH

A plant soaks up **sunlight** for energy to make its food. It needs **warmth**, which also helps its seeds to grow.

 # SPACE

Roots require enough **space** to spread out, grow deep, or even stretch upward away from soggy soil. With enough space, roots find the water and nutrients that plants need.

 # CARBON DIOXIDE

This gas is an essential ingredient used in photosynthesis, combining with water to create **glucose**. It is taken in through the **stomata** in the plant's leaves.

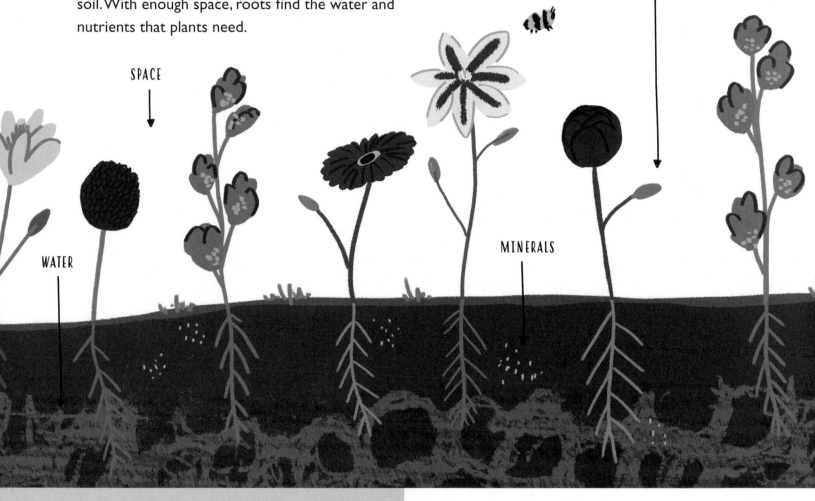

CARBON DIOXIDE

SPACE

WATER

MINERALS

 # WATER

Water is the other crucial component for photosynthesis. Plants drink it up through their roots and stem, like a straw. Some plants require lots of water to survive while others, such as a cactus in a desert, have adapted to need very little.

 # MINERALS

Plants need rich **soil** to provide them with important nutrients, including nitrogen, phosphorus, and potassium. Plants take these in through their roots.

Chapter 2

33

PLENTIFUL PLANT TYPES

Although we may think of plants as green-leafed and blossoming, there are many that do not fit this form. With hundreds of thousands of species of plants across the world, there are countless variations.

 ## GROUPED IN TWO

There are two main groups of plants: vascular and non-vascular.

 Vascular plants have special vessels for moving water and nutrients around. This group includes most of the plants on the planet.

Vascular plants are further split into groups such as flowering plants, conifers, ferns, and horsetails. There are over 260,000 different species of **flowering plants** known so far. These include orchids, sunflowers, and even peas.

Conifers, such as pines and cedars, usually have leaves shaped like needles. They grow seeds in cones that eventually drop to the ground. Conifers are usually evergreen, which means they do not drop their leaves in winter. Deciduous trees lose their leaves in winter. They have thinner, softer leaves that can't survive winter cold.

Ferns are leafy plants that reproduce by releasing **spores** from structures on the underside of their leaves called sporangia.

FERN-TASTIC!

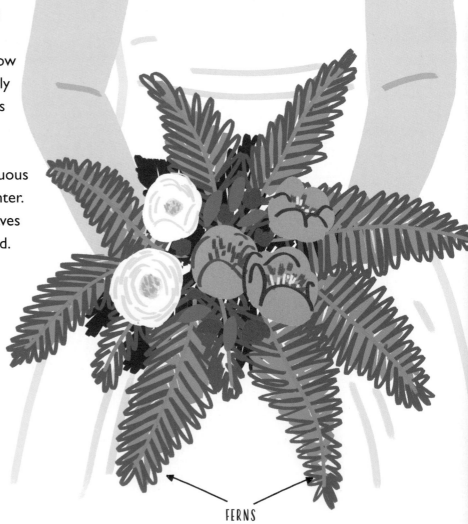

FERNS

Unlike vascular plants, **non-vascular plants** have no stems or roots, and sometimes not even true leaves. They often anchor themselves to the ground using hair-like structures called rhizoids. You might even find them on rocks or tree bark rather than in soil. These plants reproduce using spores. Non-vascular plants include mosses and green algae.

Mosses have small leaves and grow in carpets low to the ground, often in damp, shadowy places. There are over 12,000 species of moss worldwide.

Some **green algae** are tiny single cells, while other species grow to large seaweed size. They find water and grow wherever they can, whether it's in the sea or on ice.

MOSS

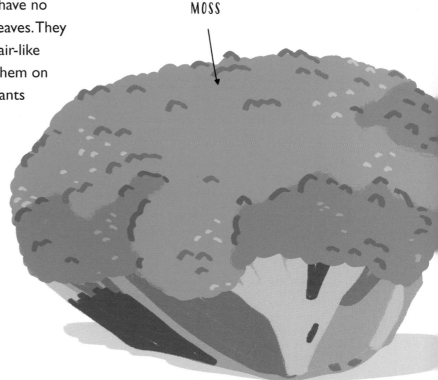

UNDERWATER SURVIVORS

We know there are plants living underwater, but how do they survive? Many aquatic plants stay close to the surface to take in sunlight. These plants, such as water lilies, often have large floating leaves. Plants deeper in the sea have adapted to require less sunlight, and they draw carbon dioxide from the water around them. No plant can live in the deep ocean, where sunlight cannot reach.

CARNIVORES

If a plant can't find what it needs in the traditional way, it might come up with creative solutions to fill in. For example, the **Venus flytrap** lives where the soil is lacking in rich nutrients. So instead, this hungry flower snatches insects and other small animals with jaw-like leaves.

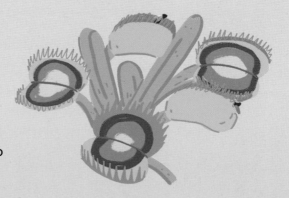

FLOWERS OF LIFE

Every living thing—plant, animal, fungus, even bacterium—has a life cycle. The life cycle of a flowering plant includes the stages of seed, plant, flower—then fruit and seeds.

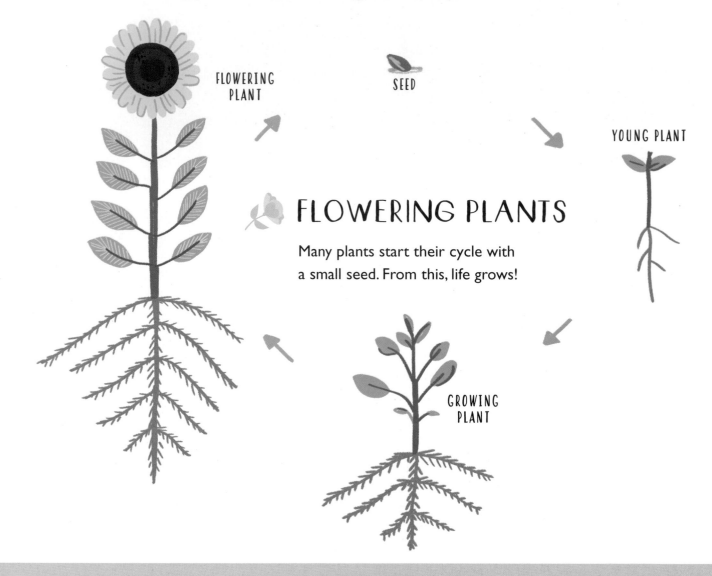

FLOWERING PLANT

SEED

YOUNG PLANT

FLOWERING PLANTS

Many plants start their cycle with a small seed. From this, life grows!

GROWING PLANT

1. A seed is dropped. It holds DNA and food that the new plant will need. This is where the plant's life begins.

2. The seed finds a home in the ground. When there is enough warmth and water, the outer case of the seed splits, and the plant starts to sprout. The roots dig into the soil and seek out nutrients. The stem pushes above the ground.

3. As the plant takes in more sunlight, water, and nutrients, leaves develop, and the plant grows taller and taller.

4. A flower grows. After the flower has been pollinated (see page 38), the seeds develop and ripen. The cycle is ready to start again.

INSIDE A FLOWER

Inside a flower are lots of little organs that help the plant live out its cycle. **Sepals** at the base protect the flower before it opens. Once it does, **petals** spread out. These are often bright to attract insects. The flower also has a **nectary**, which produces a sugary liquid called nectar, also used to attract animals. A **stamen** consists of a filament supporting an anther that holds pollen grains. A **stigma** collects grains of pollen, and an **ovary** contains **ovules** that eventually become seeds.

 # FRESH FRUIT

After **pollination**, a flower's ovules turn into seeds while its ovary turns into a fruit. Some fruits are fleshy, as in a peach, while others are hard, as in a walnut. Some fruits don't look like fruits at all! For example, dandelion fruits are feathery tufts that lift dandelion seeds on the wind. Some fruits, such as raspberries, are made of several ovaries. Not all fruits are edible (or eatable), because they are poisonous or dry. Edible fruits are very useful for spreading seeds over a large distance, as they are eaten—then pooped—by animals from birds to monkeys.

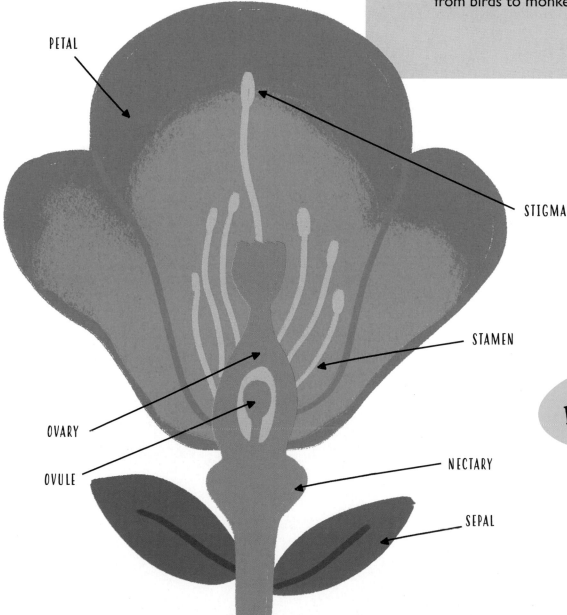

PETAL

STIGMA

STAMEN

OVARY

OVULE

INSIDE STORY!

NECTARY

SEPAL

Chapter 2

37

POWER OF POLLEN

Flowering plants, from apple trees to wheat grass, are important to our world, so it's equally important that they are able to reproduce. There are two main ways that flowering plants create this miracle of new life: sexual and asexual reproduction.

1 MALE PLUS FEMALE

Most flowering plants make their babies by **sexual reproduction**. This requires both male and female parts, which can often be found inside the same flower. The stamens are **male** parts, where pollen is produced. The pollen then needs to transfer to the **female** stigma, ovary, and ovules, usually of a different plant.

CROSS POLLINATION OF PLANTS

SELF POLLINATION

POLLINATION

Pollinators—including insects, birds, bats, and monkeys—are attracted to a flower's sweet **nectar**. When they lap it up, they brush past the pollen, which sticks to their body. As they move onto another flower, the **pollen** brushes on to the new plant's female stigma. This is called pollination. Finally, the pollen works its way down to the ovules, where **fertilization** occurs, and a seed is born.

Pollination can also be carried out by the breeze. As the wind blows, it picks up pollen and scatters it onto other flowers. A few plants, usually those living in isolated places, self-pollinate. This means that a flower is fertilized by its own pollen.

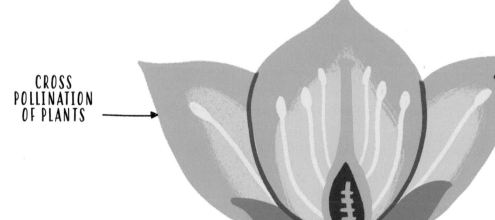
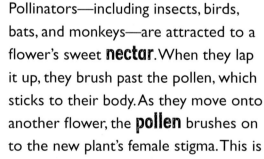

SEED DISPERSAL

Once a new seed has been produced in a fruit, it must find its way to the ground to grow into a new plant. This is called **seed dispersal**. Some seeds travel by **wind**. This is the case with key-shaped, twirling sycamore seeds. Others hitch a ride on an **animal**, either by going through the animal's digestive system (see page 37) or by attaching to the animal's fur with hooks. And some seeds, such as those of the sandbox tree, are more dramatic, **bursting** out of their fruit with little plant explosions when they're ripe.

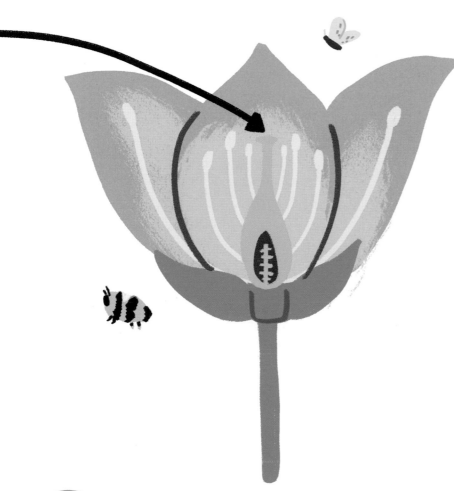

OUT OF CURIOSITY

All the tiny pollen grains floating in the wind are what cause some people to suffer from hay fever—it makes them sneeze!

GOING IT ALONE

The second type of reproduction is called **asexual reproduction**. The plant can grow new life by itself, without male and female parts or seeds. This often occurs when a human interferes, cutting off a section from the parent plant and rehoming it in rich soil, where an identical plant will grow. Some plants reproduce on their own, such as garlic or daffodils, which form large **bulbs** underground. These store food but can also split to make a new plant.

Bees are unsung heroes of the natural world. Since they pollinate many of the plants we rely on for food and materials, they are essential to human life and the **ecosystem**.

BEE

NATURE'S HEROES

Busy buzzing bees are among the key **pollinators** of many plants. In return for the sweet nectar a bee sips from a flower, the bee provides the flower with fertilization to create a new seed. It's a natural **win-win** situation. Some bees, known as **honeybees**, also produce food: honey. This is made in their stomach from the nectar they eat, then is spit back up again!

OUT OF CURIOSITY

It is only female honeybees that collect nectar and pollen. Male honeybees stay mainly in the hive.

IMPORTANT BEE

Each plant is pollinated by a particular method, such as the wind, or a small group of pollinators. Bees pollinate many common food plants, including almonds, blackberries, cabbages, onions, and potatoes. Bees also pollinate cotton and flax plants, which are widely grown to make cloth.

SMALL BUT MIGHTY

There are over **20,000** species of bee known around the world. Each one has its own specialty, and many are adapted to specific flowers. The **garden bumblebee**, for example, is the perfect pollinator for deep flowers such as honeysuckle and foxglove. It uses its long tongue to reach inside.

DANGEROUS DECLINE

The number of bees in the world is going down. Some species have disappeared entirely, and others are at risk of **extinction**. As woodland areas are cut down to build houses, or even as wildflowers are removed to make space for new crops on a farm, bees lose their homes. **Chemicals** used on plants and the planet becoming **warmer** can also have an effect on bees.

 # MAKING A DIFFERENCE

At home, we can help protect bees by planting flowers and leaving fields of wildflowers untouched. Buying honey from local farmers also supports the busy little insects that make the honey in their hives.

BOTANY AT WORK

People across the world are fascinated by the wild world of plants. They study these growing wonders and use them in everyday life in many different ways.

ON THE FARM

Agriculture is the practice of farming, both plants and animals. Plant farmers grow and harvest **crops**. These can include vegetables, fruit, wheat, cotton, and flowers. Fruit such as apples or oranges grow on trees, which are often grouped together in **orchards**. **Wheat** is an important product for flour and bread products. **Cotton** comes from plants and is used to create textiles for clothing and bedsheets, for example. Farmers need to know the intricacies of the plants they raise to give them the best conditions possible.

GROWING GARDENS

Caring for gardens is known as **horticulture**. Horticulturalists are specially trained to seek out the perfect plants for their space. They might tend to grand gardens of historical homes and need to know at what time of year different flowers grow to keep green spaces looking fresh year-round. Some horticulturalists focus on the healing properties of plants, creating gardens that are relaxing due to their sweet smell or softly swishing leaves.

 # PLANT PROTECTORS

Conservationists work to protect and preserve the environment. Forest conservationists speak up for the importance of forests—their benefits to the air, to communities, to the economy, to the ecosystem—and offer suggestions for protecting them. They fight against **deforestation** (cutting down forests) and plant new forested areas for future generations.

SAVE THE TREES!

 # NEVER STOP STUDYING

Botanists are constantly studying and learning from plants, broadening our understanding of this miraculous living world. A botanist might **breed** a new variety of plant or study the DNA of an existing one. Their work might even cross over with various fields, such as chemistry. They come up with new medicines from plant products, learn how to grow improved and modified crops, and even discover how to grow vegetables in space!

 # THE FATHER OF BOTANY

Born on a Greek island in 372 BCE, **Theophrastus** is often called the father of botany. He wrote two important book series on plants. He was the first to divide plants into systematic classifications, grouping them by location, size, use, and more. His ideas on botany were followed for hundreds of years, until later scientists refined them further.

We know that at the basic and fundamental level, plants bring us oxygen, food, and wood for building. But these multitalented superheroes have come to provide humans with much more beyond that.

PAPER PRODUCTS

It all started over 4,500 years ago, when the ancient Egyptians made the very first paper. They used papyrus, a plant similar to grass. Plants have been used in paper products ever since! Around CE 100, a printing method still used today was developed in China, taking fibrous plants rich in cellulose and putting them in water until they were reduced to a **pulp.** The water was then removed, and the pulp was pressed and dried into thin paper.

Wood from trees provides most of our paper products, which are now manufactured in huge factories. Trees can become writing paper, books, newspaper, paper money, cardboard packaging, toilet paper, and so much more in your daily life.

 ## YOUR CLOTHES

Most clothing comes from materials made from plants. After food, **cotton** is the most farmed plant product sold. About half of the **textiles** (cloth and fabric products) around the world are made of cotton. They come from the fluffy seed heads of cotton plants. Some **artificial** (human-made) textiles start with plants, too. For example, rayon is made from cellulose, which is in the cell wall of most plants. It can be made to feel like cotton or wool. Many other materials used to make textiles come from plants, too: linen, hemp, and even bamboo!

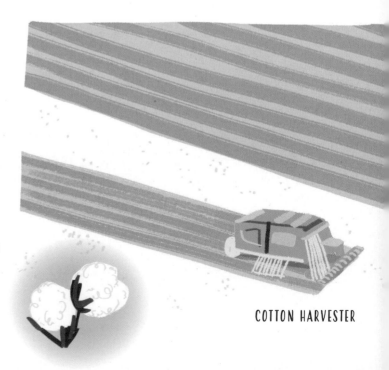

COTTON HARVESTER

HEALING POWERS

Early botanists and plant experts discovered that some plant materials could be used in **medicines**. Early plant medicines were used to help with aches and fevers. Some are still taken now. For example, people once chewed on willow bark to help with pain. It contains salicylic acid, which is made into aspirin today. Some store-bought vitamins, which may help to keep us healthy, are extracted from plants. From those relied on in the past to many new discoveries and uses today, plants have always been known to have special healing powers.

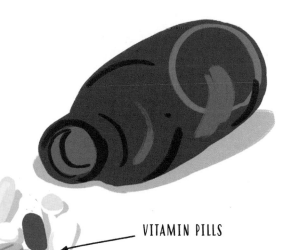

VITAMIN PILLS

FUEL THE WORLD

Much of our power comes from **fossil fuels** such as coal, oil, and natural gas. These were made over millions of years from the remains of dead plants and animals, which were buried under layers of soil and rock. However, these sources of fuel are called **non-renewable** as they cannot be replaced. They form too slowly for us to continue using them at our current rate.

It is becoming more and more important to find **renewable** sources of energy, using resources that can be replenished. These power sources include plants! For example, rather than being powered by petroleum or diesel, which are made from oil, cars can run on **biofuel**. This is a fuel created from recently harvested plants, such as sugar cane.

CHAPTER 3

ZOOLOGY: THE ANIMAL KINGDOM

As the largest kingdom of life on Earth, animals come in an incredible variety of shapes, sizes, and types. From the bottom of the sea to the harsh cold ice of Antarctica, from tropical rain forests teeming with life to vast deserts and plains, this kingdom is fascinating to explore.

Zoologists study animals: how they act, how they're grouped, and where you can find them. In this chapter, we'll go on a safari to observe the different types of animals and the various ways they survive, reproduce, and thrive in their complex worlds.

There are millions of species of animals living across the planet. A species, such as lions, is a group of animals that look similar and can make babies together. To better understand animals, scientists place species into larger groups, based on their similarities.

FAMILY TIES

All animals are related, but how closely? Classification allows scientists to group species into families and larger groups, such as orders and classes. Using features such as feathers and number of legs helps zoologists create the classifications for different animals. For example, two feathered birds are more closely related than a bird with two legs and a spider with eight! There are several groups of animals: mammals, birds, fish, reptiles, amphibians, and invertebrates. But animal similarities and differences can go even deeper than that, if you look closely.

LEOPARD VS. FENNEC FOX

FOR EXAMPLE

Let's look closely at a couple of examples to see how we can group and divide animal families:

	LEOPARD	FENNEC FOX
WARM-BLOODED?	YES	YES
HOW MANY LEGS?	FOUR	FOUR
LAYS EGGS?	NO	NO
FUR OR SCALES?	FUR	FUR
LONG MUZZLE?	NO	YES
CAN RETRACT ITS CLAWS?	YES	NO
FAMILY	CAT	DOG

The fennec fox and leopard have a lot in common, making them both mammals. However, their differences, such as the shape of their muzzle (nose and mouth) and the fact that the leopard can retract (pull back) its claws into its paws, put them in different families.

OUT OF CURIOSITY

The biggest animal ever to live on Earth is the blue whale. Its heart alone can weigh as much as a car. And yet, because both have lungs and warm blood, this massive creature can be grouped with the tiny bumblebee bat.

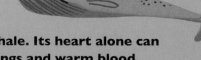

Chapter 3

48

DOES THE ANIMAL HAVE ANY HAIR?

YES → MAMMAL

NO → **DOES IT HAVE FEATHERS?**

YES → BIRD

NO → **DOES IT HAVE DRY SKIN?**

YES → REPTILE

NO → **DOES IT HAVE SCALES?**

YES → FISH

NO → AMPHIBIAN

🐾 KEY TO DISCOVERY

Next, let's look at a salamander and a hummingbird, using a **classification key**. This is a series of questions that helps identify an animal's grouping.

First, follow the key on this page for a salamander. A salamander has no hair, no feathers, no dry skin, and no scales, which leads you to the group **AMPHIBIAN**. Now follow the same key for a hummingbird. As it has no hair, but it does have feathers, you should arrive at **BIRD**. These animals are of two very different groups.

VARIOUS VERTEBRATES

The millions of animal species around the world are divided into two core groups based on one main feature: whether or not they have a backbone. Within each group, the animal species are further broken down.

SUN BEAR

BONE STRUCTURES

The first of the two main classifications for animals is **vertebrates**. Every animal in this group has a **backbone**: the series of bones that run down the back, from the base of the neck to the tailbone. The backbone protects the vital nerves of the **spinal cord** and gives the organism **structure**. The animals in this group are divided into five categories.

MAMMALS

The class of **mammals** has the smallest number of species, but the most diverse. It includes lions, dolphins, sun bears, rabbits—and humans! Mammals all have warm blood and hair or fur. Even dolphins and whales have whiskers. Mammals usually give birth to live young and feed their young on milk.

REPTILES

CHAMELEON

Reptiles are cold-blooded, so they take in heat from the sun and from their own muscles, and then seek out shade if they get too hot. Most reptiles lay eggs, although some, like certain snakes, give birth to live young. All reptiles have dry scales or bonier plates called scutes. They can have four legs or none at all. This group includes tortoises, chameleons, snakes, and crocodiles.

SCARLET MACAW

🦴 BIRDS

Birds are descended from a group of small, feathered dinosaurs, which were reptiles that lived millions of years ago. Birds have feathers and wings. Most birds can fly, although some use their wings to help them swim or balance on land instead. Birds lay hard-shelled eggs and are warm-blooded. This group includes sparrows, eagles, parrots, penguins, and the tall ostrich.

TOAD

🦴 AMPHIBIANS

Amphibians live on land and in water. Most have four legs, which they use to walk or swim. Most amphibians start their lives in a different form, called larvae, in water, taking in oxygen from the water using structures called gills. When amphibians grow into adults, they usually develop lungs and legs and live on land. They have moist skin, cold blood, and lay soft-shelled eggs. This group includes frogs, toads, salamanders, and newts.

CLOWNFISH

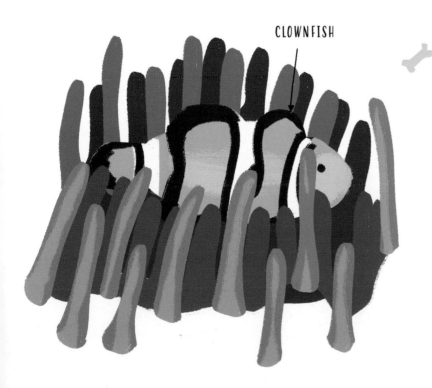

🦴 FISH

Finally, the largest group by far! **Fish** were the very first animals to develop a backbone, and there are now over 30,000 different species of fish across the world. They all live in water and use gills to take in oxygen from the water. Almost all fish have scales. Most fish lay soft eggs, while others, such as sharks, give birth to live young. This group includes goldfish, clownfish, eels, and the great white shark.

Chapter 3

51

WORLD OF INVERTEBRATES

Around 97% of animals on Earth are **invertebrates**. They have no backbone and instead have completely soft bodies or hard outer casings. They are divided into more than 30 groups. Here are some common ones.

INSECTS

This group has a couple of claims to fame. First, it is the largest group of animals on Earth. And second, it was the first to fly! **Insects** have six legs, a three-part body, a pair of antennae (feelers), and a hard **exoskeleton** (skeleton on the outside of the body). Many also have wings. This group includes everything from beetles to butterflies to the ruthless praying mantis.

BUTTERFLY

JAPANESE SPIDER CRAB

CRUSTACEANS

Crustaceans are closely related to insects. They have hard shells and jointed legs. They live mostly in water, although some, such as woodlice, live on land. Many have claws, which they use to grip things or defend themselves. They range from little krill to the giant Japanese spider crab.

SPIDER

COMMON OCTOPUS

🦋 ARACHNIDS

Most **arachnids** have two body sections and eight legs. They live on land or in water. Arachnids have a hard outer shell, but, unlike insects, they have no antennae or wings. They are mostly predators and have several pairs of eyes to see prey. This group includes mites, ticks, spiders, and scorpions.

🦋 MOLLUSKS

Mollusks range greatly in size and shape. They include oysters, clams, octopus, snails, and the giant squid. All have a soft body, and many have a hard outer shell for protection. Most are found in water and swim around or crawl. Some animals in this group, such as slugs, do not have a central brain, while others, such as octopus, have quite large brains. Octopus can build dens from rocks and shells, hide from predators, and ambush their prey.

SEA ANEMONE

🦋 CNIDARIANS

Cnidarians can be found only in water. They spend part of their early life as a sessile (unmoving) cylinder-shaped polyp. As they reach adulthood, some cnidarians change body shape so they are able to swim. All cnidarians have stinging cells, which they can use to capture prey or defend themselves against predators. This group includes coral, sea anemones, and jellyfish.

LIFE CYCLES

Just like plants and other life forms, every animal goes through a life cycle. It is born, grows older and bigger, possibly has children of its own, and eventually dies. Its children might have their own children, and the cycle continues.

VARIETIES OF ANIMAL LIFE

Animals hatch from eggs or are born as live babies. Some animals look like their parents when they're born, while others go through a major change before they become adults. Each animal has its own unique life cycle.

NEWBORN CUB

YOUNG LION

ADULT LION

GROWING UP

Most mammals are born live from their mothers. They look similar to their parents when they emerge, but grow bigger as they age. Mammals provide milk for their young until they are able to find their own food. Humans take care of their babies for longer than any other species, in part because we are totally helpless at birth and then develop very slowly. Most mammals have shorter life cycles than humans. For example, a lion cub begins walking by 10 days old. By three or four years old it can have its own babies.

SPREADING WINGS

Many insects start their life as a **larva**—a newly hatched creature, which in insects often looks like a small worm. The larva fills up on food and grows bigger, sometimes shedding an outer skin as it does so. Once it is big enough, it becomes a **pupa**, or **chrysalis**. The insect spends the pupa stage sheltered in a cocoon or protected by a case, not moving while it changes shape.

EGG

CATERPILLAR (LARVA)

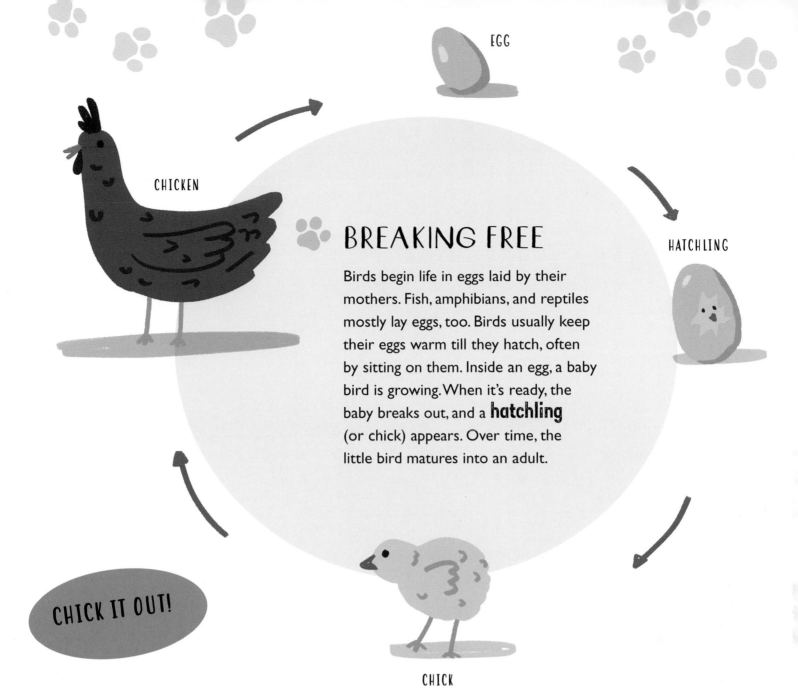

CHICKEN

EGG

HATCHLING

BREAKING FREE

Birds begin life in eggs laid by their mothers. Fish, amphibians, and reptiles mostly lay eggs, too. Birds usually keep their eggs warm till they hatch, often by sitting on them. Inside an egg, a baby bird is growing. When it's ready, the baby breaks out, and a **hatchling** (or chick) appears. Over time, the little bird matures into an adult.

CHICK IT OUT!

CHICK

Inside, its body changes—a process called **metamorphosis**. Eventually the adult form emerges.

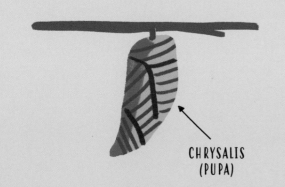

CHRYSALIS
(PUPA)

BUTTERFLY

Animals must reproduce in order to keep their species alive. Some animals have lots of babies to ensure survival, while others focus on just one baby at a time. Each animal has its own way of reproducing.

MAKING BABIES

Nearly all animals need a **male** and a **female** to reproduce. They must **mate** for a baby to begin to grow. For mammals such as sheep, giraffes, and humans, the baby begins to grow inside the female, and she is **pregnant**. The baby is born into the world when it has developed enough to be able to survive.

IN MOTHER'S POUCH

A group of mammals called **marsupials** give birth to babies that are small and not very well developed. Once the baby is born, it goes straight into a pouch on the mother's body to continue growing and developing until it is ready to emerge into the world on its own. Kangaroos, koalas, and wombats all have these practical pouches.

PRECIOUS EGGS

For most reptiles, insects, fish, and birds, the female lays **eggs** for babies to develop outside her body within a safe space. While most birds watch over their eggs, most reptiles leave their eggs to develop on their own. Fish lay as many as several thousand jelly-like eggs in water, then swim away. A few fish look after their eggs until they hatch. For example, the male jawfish holds a female's eggs in his mouth till the babies are born.

EGG-CELLENT!

OUT OF CURIOSITY

Some baby animals have a special egg tooth that they can use to help them break out of their shell.

ANIMAL EXCEPTIONS

As always, some animals behave differently than others related to them. The platypus is one of only five mammals, known as **monotremes**, that lay eggs. This fact, along with its beak, webbed feet, fur, and venomous sting puzzled scientists when it was first discovered! Some snake species give birth to live young, while others lay eggs. Some can even do a combination of **both**, keeping the eggs inside the body until they are ready to hatch.

Chapter 3

57

FOLLOWING FOOD CHAINS

Every animal needs to eat. Without food, it would have no energy, and without energy, it couldn't survive. Some organisms can make their own food, but animals can't. This is where food chains come in.

 ## CHAIN OF COMMAND

A **food chain**, like the one on page 59, shows a series of organisms that depend on each other for food. Every food chain starts with a **producer**. These are the organisms that can produce their own food, such as plants. Everything that eats something else in the chain is called a **consumer**.

The first consumers in the chain are called the **primary consumers.** If they eat only plants, they are **herbivores**. The animals that eat the primary consumers are the **secondary consumers**. The animals next in line are the **tertiary consumers**. These animals that eat other animals are called **carnivores**. Some animals are happy to eat either meat or plants, and they are called **omnivores**.

ENERGY PYRAMID

SHARK

TUNA

HERRING

KRILL

PHYTOPLANKTON

HUNTER OR HUNTED

In nature, animals must seek out their own food in whatever way they can to survive. Many animals hunt for their meals. They are **predators**. The animals that they hunt are their **prey**. If an owl eats a mouse, the owl is the predator and the mouse is its prey.

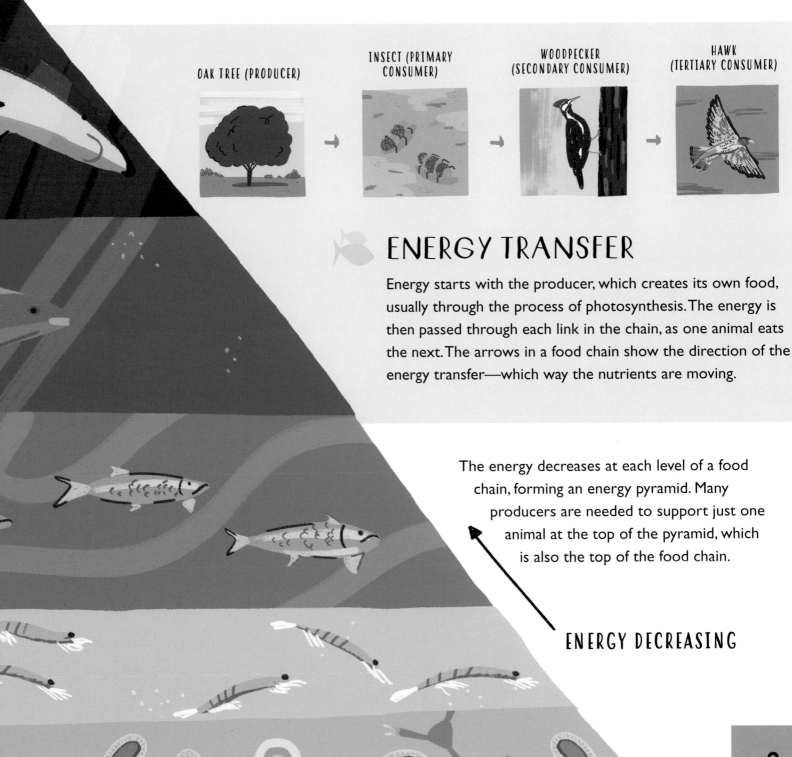

OAK TREE (PRODUCER) → INSECT (PRIMARY CONSUMER) → WOODPECKER (SECONDARY CONSUMER) → HAWK (TERTIARY CONSUMER)

ENERGY TRANSFER

Energy starts with the producer, which creates its own food, usually through the process of photosynthesis. The energy is then passed through each link in the chain, as one animal eats the next. The arrows in a food chain show the direction of the energy transfer—which way the nutrients are moving.

The energy decreases at each level of a food chain, forming an energy pyramid. Many producers are needed to support just one animal at the top of the pyramid, which is also the top of the food chain.

ENERGY DECREASING

CHOMPING DINNER

Animals take in food, extract energy and nutrients, then get rid of
anything not needed. Different animals eat different diets,
and their bodies are suited to their feeding style.

IN AND OUT

Most animals take in food through their mouth. It then travels through their body, where energy
is absorbed. This is called **digestion**. Any waste (parts of the food not needed) leaves the body.

Humans and many other mammals, such as dogs and rhinos, have a digestive
system that is **monogastric**. This means they have one stomach. They can
eat solid food high in energy. In contrast, some mammals, such as cows and
giraffes, have four stomach compartments. This is a **ruminant** digestive system.
In the first two compartments, low-energy plant material is broken down into solids and
liquids, then the solids are brought up into the mouth and rechewed. Digestion is helped
by microorganisms, such as bacteria, in the next compartments, which break down the
tough material to get the most energy from it. This type of stomach is not needed to
digest high-energy food and protein.

SUPER STOMACH

🐤 TOOTHLESS

Birds, such as chickens and flamingos, have a different system again: an **avian** digestive system. They have no teeth and instead peck up food with their beaks. Some also eat small pebbles or sand to help crush the food inside. Their stomachs have one part like a human's stomach, and another part called the **gizzard**. The gizzard is a muscular **organ** that works with the pebbles or sand to grind up the food before the nutrients are eventually absorbed.

🐤 TYPE OF TEETH

Herbivores and carnivores have very differently shaped teeth. Herbivores use **flat, rounded** teeth to squash and grind the plants they eat. Carnivores have **sharp, pointed** teeth to slice and rip up meat. Sharks have multiple rows of up to 3,000 teeth, ready to replace any that they lose. Some are pointed backward so prey can't escape once inside their mouth.

OUT OF CURIOSITY

Flamingos are born with fluffy white feathers. They turn pink as they grow due to all the pink shrimp and algae that they eat!

Chapter 3

61

SELECTION OF SKELETONS

A **skeleton** is the framework of bones and cartilage that supports and protects an organism's body. Some animals have a skeleton on the inside, some on the outside, and some not at all!

ON THE INSIDE

All vertebrates, such as humans, horses, frogs, and fish, have a skeleton inside their body. This is called an **endoskeleton**. It supports and holds up the body, while also protecting all the delicate organs inside. As the organism grows, the endoskeleton grows, too. The human body has over 200 bones in its skeleton. A snake can have up to 600!

ON THE OUTSIDE

Many invertebrates have skeletons on the outside of their body, rather than the inside. This is called an **exoskeleton**. It provides a rigid outer structure and protection for invertebrates such as crabs, lobsters, and spiders. As the animal grows, it sheds its exoskeleton and forms a new one to replace it. A grasshopper might go through around five exoskeletons in its lifetime.

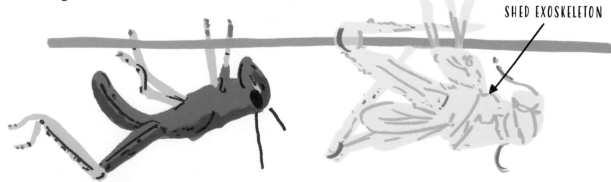

SHED EXOSKELETON

Some mollusks, such as clams and snails, have a hard **shell** instead of an exoskeleton. It protects their soft body and gives them a place to hide from danger. This shell grows with them by expanding along its edges.

SHELL

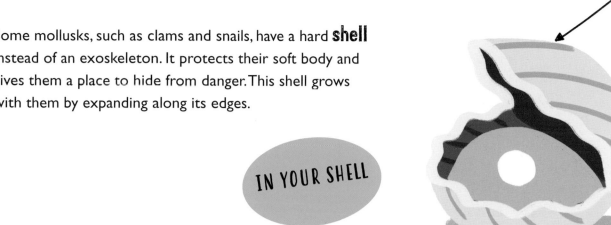

IN YOUR SHELL

ENDOSKELETON

GOING WITHOUT

Some animals have neither an exoskeleton nor an endoskeleton. These invertebrates include jellyfish and worms. However, they do have a **hydrostatic skeleton**, or **hydro skeleton**. Fluid inside their bodies holds their shape and helps them move.

CHARLES DARWIN

Charles Darwin was born in England in 1809. Throughout his life, he studied animals, plants, and rocks. He made many observations about living creatures and **evolution** (the way living things change over time), including one fascinating fact based on skeletons. He noticed that all four-limbed animals, such as dogs, humans, and even dolphins, had the same bone structure in their limbs. This led him to the conclusion that all four-limbed animals had the **same ancestor** millions of years ago. This means that you can say you are related to a *Tyrannosaurus rex!*

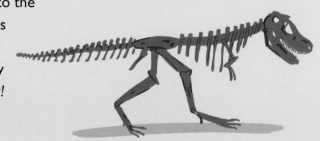

STRIVING FOR SURVIVAL

The ultimate goal of an animal is to survive. Each animal has special skills and tricks to find food and escape from predators.

SURVIVAL

Every living thing has a drive to survive. Humans eat, find safety, and take shelter. But in the wild animal kingdom, creatures must fight for their lives—and not only their own lives, but also the lives of their babies. To rise to this challenge, some animals rely on strong hunting skills. They are on the **offensive**. Other animals survive with strategies to protect or hide themselves. They are on the **defensive**. Many animals must both attack and defend.

DEFENSIVE TACTICS

If an animal is threatened, it might need to defend itself. Many animals would prefer to avoid a fight, so they try to scare off attackers instead. Some animals, such as giant armadillos, rear up on their hind legs to look taller and menacing. Others puff up, fluff out their feathers, or spread their ears. A frilled lizard has a crest around its neck that it can flare to scare. The Virginia opossum has a completely different tactic: it pretends to be dead when it is threatened, as most of its predators don't want to eat rotting meat.

VICIOUS VENOM

Venoms are poisonous liquids that can be used as defensive or offensive tactics. The golden dart frog makes venom that it releases through its skin. This makes it one of the most poisonous animals in the world if it is eaten. The frog's bright golden skin warns that it is deadly. In contrast, the rattlesnake uses its venom to catch prey. When it bites its target, it releases venom through sharp hollow teeth called fangs. The venom disables the prey, ready to eat.

GOLDEN DART FROG

FEELING PRICKLY

Some animals have weapons that give more of a warning than a deadly sting. A porcupine, for example, has stiff, sharp quills that raise when the animal is threatened. If an attacker comes too close, the porcupine throws some quills out and they stick to the attacker. Ouch! The porcupine grows new quills to replace any that are lost.

RAISING A STINK

Other animals can literally raise a stink to scare off attackers. A skunk can release a bad-smelling liquid from the base of its tail. It can spray this on a target up to 4 m (13 ft) away—the length of a small car.

SKUNK

HIDE AND SEEK

Camouflage is a tactic used by many animals in the wild. These animals have **evolved** to blend into their surroundings. The chameleon is one of the animals most famous for its camouflaging capabilities. It switches through various shades to hide in plain sight among leaves or flowers. Other animals change seasonally. For example, an Arctic hare is brown in the summer, to hide around rocks. In the winter, however, it turns almost pure white to blend in with the snow.

ARCTIC HARE

CHAPTER 4

ECOLOGY: HABITATS AND CO-HABITATION

Across our planet, the weather and landscapes vary greatly. Ice and cold dominate the poles, while the regions around the equator have hot weather year round. Yet from poles to equator, mountaintops to deserts, living things make their homes. Different species have adapted over time to different temperatures and terrains.

Ecology is the study of how organisms relate to each other and their particular environment. This includes where creatures live, how the **climate** affects them, how they interact with others in the same space, and human effects on their home. As you travel through this chapter, think about the living things in your local habitats, whether that is city streets or farmland.

HABITATS AROUND THE WORLD

A **habitat** is the place where an animal, plant, or other living thing makes its home. A creature's habitat is where it finds food and shelter. Habitats range from deserts to ponds, rotting logs to rainforests.

🏠 HOME SWEET HOME

Each living thing is suited to the habitat where it lives. In its habitat, the organism can find its food, suitable shelter, and the right levels of sunlight and water.

African bush elephants, for example, move between African savanna and forest habitats. Their bodies are suited to eating the grass, leaves, and bark they find there. They are also suited to the climate, which has a rainy season and a dry season. Climate is a region's usual long-term weather pattern. In dry seasons, elephants use their tusks to dig up riverbeds and create new waterholes. Elephants also **interact** with the living things that share their habitat. Elephant dung spreads plant seeds—while dung beetles lay their eggs in it!

🏠 CLIMATE CONTROL

In each habitat, the food and shelter—from trees to grasses—are dependent on the climate and the wider **environment**. If the climate changes, food and shelter might become less readily available. Diseases, natural disasters, and human activities might also affect a creature's access to resources. Eventually, creatures may need to find a new habitat if their habitat changes too much or too fast.

FEELING AT HOME!

WATER CYCLE

Habitats vary across the world depending on how much sunlight and **water** they get. Areas with plenty of rain, such as rainforests, are full of plant and animal life. Dry deserts have fewer residents, which are all adapted to live with the limited water. The water on Earth is constantly moving and recycled in what is called the **water cycle**.

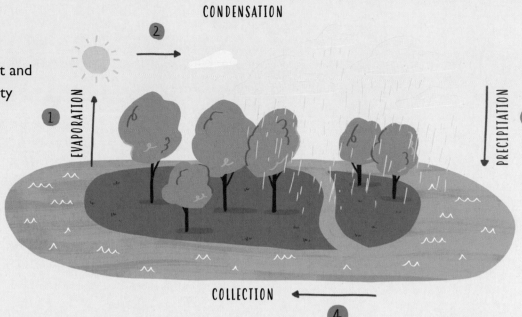

CONDENSATION

EVAPORATION

PRECIPITATION

COLLECTION

1. The sun **evaporates** water in lakes, rivers, and oceans. The water turns to vapor and rises into the air.

2. Water vapor in the sky cools down and **condenses** into little water droplets, which we see as clouds.

3. The droplets in the cloud get heavy, so the water drops back to Earth as rain or snow. This is called **precipitation**.

4. The rain runs across the land and into rivers, which carry it back to the ocean. This is **collection**, and the cycle begins again.

BIOMES

From deserts to grasslands, oceans to forests, Planet Earth has a wide range of **biomes**. A biome is a large community of life that is suited to a geographic region and climate.

BEAUTIFUL BIOMES

Similar biomes are found in different regions across the world. For example, the temperate forest biome is found in Europe, North America, and many other places. A biome can contain lots of different habitats. Habitats in a temperate forest include fallen leaves and tree branches.

Scientists divide Earth into anywhere between five and twenty biomes. These are some of the common ones.

BIOME TO BIOME

Polar biome: With the slippery ice and extreme cold, not just any creature can live in polar regions. In fact, some animals migrate to warmer climates when the temperature drops in winter. Others, including penguins and polar bears, thrive in these harsh lands at the top and bottom of the world.

Tropical forest: This warm, wet habitat is home to more species than any other biome. Trees stretch to the sky for sunlight, creating sunny habitats in their canopy and shadowy habitats below. Rain forests teem with animal, plant, and fungus life.

Temperate forest: This biome is full of trees, both with broad, flat leaves (deciduous trees) and with needle-like leaves (evergreen trees). The region has four seasons a year, and the leaves of deciduous trees follow, growing, changing, and falling in an endless cycle. Many animals eat the seeds, nuts, leaves, and berries provided by the trees.

Mountains: Within the mountains, there can be several habitats. The valleys host woodlands, while the slopes are covered by evergreens. On tall mountaintops, the climate is cold and windy. Very few plants live on the peaks—only those lower to the ground, such as mosses, can survive.

Desert: In the driest biome, animals and plants, such as cacti, have special features to store water for long periods of time. Deserts may be hot or cold, depending on their distance from the equator. In hot deserts, many animals hide under rocks or in burrows to escape the daytime heat, then come out in the cooler night to feast.

Grassland: With more rainfall than deserts but less than forests, grasslands are mainly covered in grasses. Grasses need less rain than tall trees. Grass provides food to herds of herbivores, who in turn are the perfect prey for carnivores such as lions. Grasslands are found across the world, with different names such as savannas, prairies, or pampas.

Water: Biomes are also found in the water that covers two-thirds of our planet. These biomes can be fresh water or salty oceans. At least one million animal species live in the oceans, ranging from tiny plankton to large whales. Habitats in the ocean biome range from sunlit coral reefs to the dark seafloor.

WORKING TOGETHER

No living thing can survive on its own.
It takes a whole team of plants and animals—as well as
many non-living elements—to keep the community thriving.

ECOSYSTEM EFFORT

The interaction between the living and non-living things in a habitat is called an **ecosystem**. Energy, nutrients, and other materials travel through an ecosystem. An ecosystem needs every element to be in **perfect balance**. An ecosystem can exist in a single tree trunk, a rock pool, or a vast forest. Every part of the ecosystem affects others, from a single animal species to the carbon dioxide in the air.

TREE-MENDOUS TEAMWORK

Each organism within an ecosystem has its own habitat. But organisms cannot exist on their own—they all **interact** with others in the community. For example, insects living in a tree use the leaves as food, while birds use the branches for shelter.

REUSE AND RECYCLE

Alongside the life in an ecosystem are resources such as air, water, and soil. A key element in ecosystems is **recycling**. Nutrients, energy, and water all go through processes to be reused to continue supporting the community. For example, when an animal dies, its body decays into the soil, leaving nutrients that help plants grow.

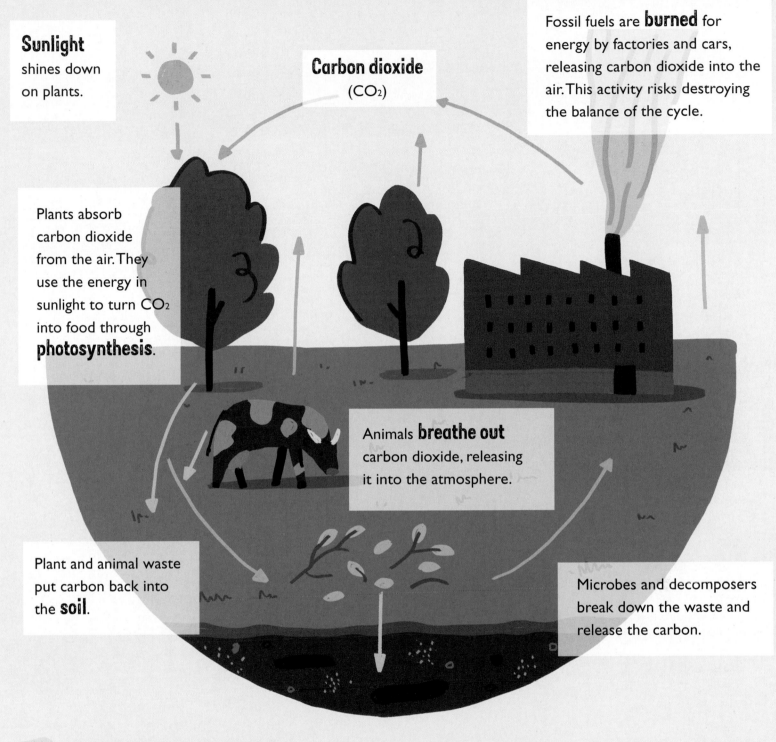

Sunlight shines down on plants.

Carbon dioxide (CO₂)

Fossil fuels are **burned** for energy by factories and cars, releasing carbon dioxide into the air. This activity risks destroying the balance of the cycle.

Plants absorb carbon dioxide from the air. They use the energy in sunlight to turn CO₂ into food through **photosynthesis**.

Animals **breathe out** carbon dioxide, releasing it into the atmosphere.

Plant and animal waste put carbon back into the **soil**.

Microbes and decomposers break down the waste and release the carbon.

CARBON CYCLE

One of the key essential elements in all ecosystems is **carbon**. It is constantly used and **recycled** through plants, animals, and air to support life on Earth. The **carbon cycle** is carefully balanced naturally, but by burning fossil fuels humans are disrupting it.

VARIETY OF LIFE

Life can be found in every corner of the world—but some corners have a broader range of life than others! This is important to understand for the long-term protection of our planet.

RANGE OF LIFE

Biodiversity is the variety of life in a particular area. For example, a rainforest gets plenty of warmth and rain, so it is able to support many different living things: it has a **high biodiversity** of animals and plants. At the other end of the spectrum, a polar region has **low biodiversity**—the harsh conditions mean there are fewer species living there. Areas with high biodiversity are more **stable** and can withstand changes to their ecosystem better than other areas.

RICH RAINFOREST

The Amazon rainforest is home to millions of species of insects, reptiles, birds, plants, and other life forms. It is one of the most biodiverse places on the planet.

OUT OF CURIOSITY

In the rainforest, the leaves and trees are so closely packed that it can take 10 minutes for rainwater to reach the ground.

EMERGENT LAYER

At the top of the forest, the tallest trees can reach 60 m (200 ft) from the ground. This layer receives the most sunlight. Here, you can find soaring birds and bright butterflies soaking up the sun.

CANOPY

Most animals of the rainforest live in this dense layer of treetops. This includes sloths, monkeys, toucans, and tree frogs. Many rarely go down to the forest floor, as they have everything they need to survive in the trees.

UNDERSTORY

This layer gets a lot less light than the canopy. Small bushes with large leaves provide shelter for animals ranging from bats to snakes.

FOREST FLOOR

With very little light able to pass through the branches to the ground, the forest floor is dark but damp. Insects, spiders, and mammals such as anteaters find their food and homes here.

In any habitat, many living creatures exist alongside each other, carrying on with their own lives. But animals cannot make their own food, so they must feed on other living things. Each animal's life links with others.

FOOD WEBS

A **food chain** is a series of animals and plants that depend on each other for food. Nutrients and energy pass through the chain, from the producer at the bottom to the final link at the top. A polar bear's food chain could look like this, for example:

PLANKTON → SHRIMP → SEAL → POLAR BEAR

A **food web** shows how different food chains link together in one ecosystem. One organism could provide food to animals in several different chains. The web shows how they all interact.

The Arctic food web to the right includes the polar bear's food chain above, but also shows how it is joined with others. We can see that the orca and polar bear compete for the same meal sometimes. In this food web, both the orca and polar bear are **apex predators**. This means that they are top of the food chain—nothing eats them unless they are sick, very young, or already dead.

COD

PLANKTON

SHRIMP

CONNECTIONS

The various food chains in a food web are closely connected, so what happens if one part of the web changes? If the plankton disappeared, for example, the whole food web could break down. The cod and shrimp would have little food to eat and would either need to move to another habitat or die out. And if their population decreased, then the animals at the top of the food chain would be in danger of starvation as well. Every food chain is a precarious balancing act.

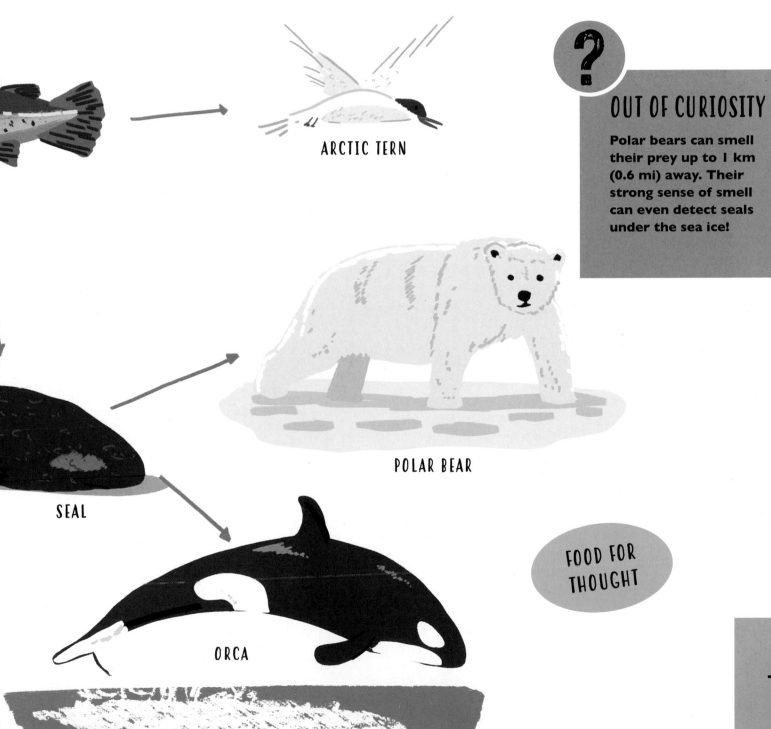

ARCTIC TERN

POLAR BEAR

SEAL

ORCA

OUT OF CURIOSITY

Polar bears can smell their prey up to 1 km (0.6 mi) away. Their strong sense of smell can even detect seals under the sea ice!

FOOD FOR THOUGHT

ENVIRONMENTS OF CHANGE

People often say that one of the only things that stays the same in life is, in fact, change. In the living world, environments are always changing, sometimes slowly over the long history of the planet, and sometimes very quickly.

⚖ KEEPING THE BALANCE

An ecosystem is a delicate interconnected web of species and resources. These species interact with and rely on each other. Resources in the ecosystem must be enough to keep each creature going. If they are not, or if they suddenly disappear, the balance of the whole system can fall apart.

⚖ KEY TO LIFE

There are several creatures that are absolutely essential to the survival of the whole ecosystem. They are called **keystone species**. These organisms hold the system together, and without them, the ecosystem would change or die. A keystone species could be a predator, such as a shark. Sharks eat small fish, which in turn keeps these small fish from eating all the sea grass.

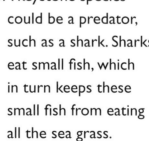

Keystone species might also be **eco engineers** (which make changes to the landscape), such as a beaver. The beaver builds dams, removing dead trees from woodland and making way for new ones. Their dams also redirect water into new wetlands for other animals and plants. Without them, many animals would have no home.

BUSY BEAVERS!

NATURAL DISASTERS

Natural disasters are huge events that happen in nature. They can have catastrophic effects on people, plants, and animals.

Volcanoes can wipe out whole habitats. Eventually, once conditions are more stable, new species that can survive in harsh climates will move in and begin making new habitats. A forest might grow back within 150 years, if there are no more eruptions.

Wildfires travel fast and leave destruction in their wake. They can be caused by a dangerous mixture of too little water, too much heat, and lightning. Once a fire starts, it can travel through the forest faster than 20 km/h (12 mph)—nearly as fast as a running bull. Animals might be unable to escape, or they may flee. For example, if there are bushfires in Australia, many koalas lose their homes and flee into cities. Eventually, the forest regrows for new life to move in.

Tsunamis are huge waves that can flood the land. They are caused by underwater earthquakes or volcanic eruptions and can wipe out life along the coasts they hit. They can also affect underwater ecosystems. For example, if coral reef fish are disturbed, the reef sharks that eat them must look elsewhere.

The Earth's climate naturally changes over time. Much of the planet was covered in ice in the past! But lately, Earth's temperature has been rising faster than ever before.

CLIMATE CHANGE

The process of our planet heating up is called **climate change**, or global heating. Scientists estimate that in the last 140 years, Earth's average temperature has risen by 1°C (2°F). That may not sound like a big amount, but it can have huge effects on habitats and living things around the world.

CAUSES

Earth's climate has always changed. But the reason the change has sped up more recently is due to one creature—humans. While we take land to expand cities and use more and more fossil fuels, the planet suffers.

Fossil fuels: When we burn fossil fuels such as oil and coal, carbon dioxide is released into the atmosphere. This gas works like a blanket around Earth, trapping the Sun's heat and warming the planet. This is called the **greenhouse effect**.

Carbon dioxide: We know that **carbon** is an essential element for life, but it exists in a delicate carbon cycle that ensures there isn't too much of it in the air. Lately, more carbon dioxide (CO_2) is being added to the atmosphere than can be taken away. Carbon dioxide is a powerful greenhouse gas. In addition, when humans cut down forests, we remove one of the main helpers that takes carbon dioxide out of the air.

Farming: Farming meat affects the planet. Cows, for example, eat grass and then release gas from their mouths or bottoms. This is a **greenhouse gas** called **methane**—and when 1.5 billion cows around the world let it out, it can seriously affect the atmosphere!

EFFECTS

The world is warming up faster than some living things can adapt to keep up. The rising temperature causes changes in the weather, which in turn affects wildlife around the globe.

Weather: As the world heats up, the weather is becoming more extreme and unpredictable. Rainfall and floods during storms are increasing in some areas, while droughts (or long periods without rain) are worsening in other areas. Sea ice is melting, causing sea levels to rise and affecting coastal habitats.

Wildlife: As the weather and landscapes change, animals' homes change, too. For example, in the Arctic, as sea ice melts, polar bears lose their hunting and resting space. On warmer coasts, sea turtles lose their nesting beaches as water levels rise. Flowers and the times they bloom change, affecting the birds and insects that depend on them. Every link in an ecosystem feels the effects of a warmer planet.

MELTING SEA ICE

HUMAN IMPACT

Humans are impacting the planet more than any other species.
There are so many of us that we have immense power to do
harm—or good—to all the habitats on Earth.

DEFORESTATION

Across the world, humans cut down
forests to make space for new homes,
roads, factories, farms, mines, and more.
Suddenly, trees that were taking carbon
dioxide out of the air are no longer
there. This means that more CO_2 stays
in the atmosphere, helping to heat up
the planet.

Deforestation also takes homes from
wildlife. Jaguars once roamed from the
southern United States all the way
down to Argentina, but today their
habitat has been cut in half. They now
stay mainly in the Amazon rainforest.

LOGGING TRUCK

SEA TURTLE

PLASTIC WASTE

A plastic bottle thrown aside may join
the 8 million tonnes (8.8 US tons)
of plastic that enter the oceans every
year. Wind or rain carries the litter to
drains, rivers, or streams. These lead to
the ocean, where a fish might eat the
plastic waste. Then, the larger fish that
eats that little fish also swallows the
plastic. Plastic can fill a fish's stomach,
stopping it from eating food. Plastic can
also trap an animal's fin, making it hard
for them to swim and survive.

POLLUTION

Burning fossil fuels for power or transport **pollutes** the planet. In addition to worsening global warming, air pollution—in the form of small particles and gases such as ozone and carbon monoxide—can worsen asthma in humans. Air pollution can also make rain more acidic, which can affect freshwater habitats such as ponds and lakes.

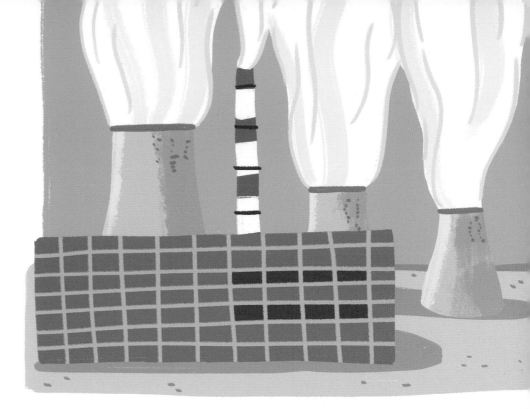

POWER PLANT

 # CHAIN REACTION

In the twentieth century, prairie dogs were removed from **98%** of their habitat in the United States—because farmers saw them as pests. The problem was that, without prairie dogs, the black-footed ferret, their main predator, had no food to eat. The black-footed ferret, in turn, nearly became **extinct**. Today, conservationists are working to protect and breed both prairie dogs and black-footed ferrets to help their numbers grow again.

PRAIRIE DOGS

PROTECTING OUR ENVIRONMENT

Humans can disrupt ecosystems, but we can also help protect them.
Our actions can preserve wildlife, as well as the planet that we call home.

CLEAN ENERGY

Fossil fuels, such as coal and oil, pollute the atmosphere. A huge way to help the planet is to replace these with cleaner sources of power. These include natural resources, such as sunlight and wind, that also have the benefit of never running out. Sunlight can be absorbed using **solar panels**, which turn the Sun's energy into electricity that can be used to power machines or heat homes. Wind can also generate electricity through large **wind turbines** that harness the power of the breeze. They turn movement energy into electrical energy.

WIND TURBINES

RECYCLING

Materials such as paper, metal, glass, textiles, and plastics can be **recycled**, by being processed and reformed into new products or packaging. Recycling reduces the waste that is buried or burned, and cuts the quantity of resources and fuel used making objects from raw materials. We can also reduce the amount of waste we produce, by reusing products when possible and choosing products with less packaging.

GOING GREEN

Planting new woodland areas introduces new trees to absorb carbon dioxide from the air. On a smaller scale, you can grow some of your own vegetables and other plants at home, and buy food that's been grown near where you live. You won't be able to grow enough for all of your needs, but every plant helps to take carbon dioxide out of the air, and reduces the number of trucks and planes needed to get food to stores.

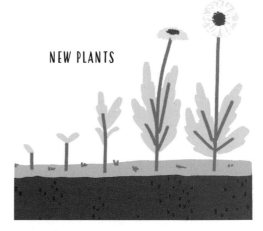

NEW PLANTS

SPECIES PROTECTION

When species become **endangered**, humans sometimes step in to help—but often humans were responsible in the first place, by destroying an organism's habitat, or hunting it. The pangolin has been hunted for its scales and meat. This has caused its numbers to drop rapidly, moving it toward extinction. Governments have introduced laws to protect the species, but it may not be enough. More and more species are becoming endangered.

PANGOLIN

ELECTRIC POWER

To replace gasoline and diesel, which release CO_2 into the air, scientists have invented cars that run on **electricity**. These electric cars use batteries for power and can be plugged in to recharge. Researchers believe electric cars will eventually replace those that run on fossil fuels, cutting down CO_2 emissions, as long as the electricity doesn't come from coal-powered power stations.

ELECTRIC CAR

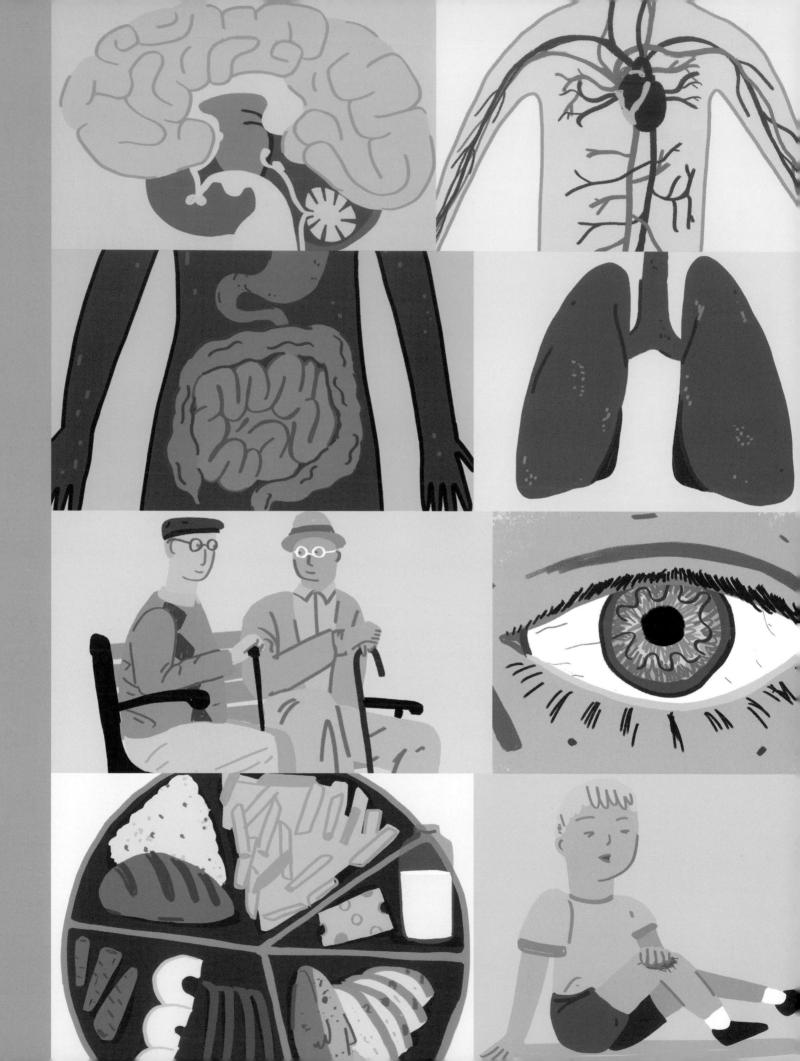

CHAPTER 5

ANATOMY: THE HUMAN BODY

The human body is like a well-oiled machine. A magnificent, miraculous machine. Many parts work together to create a living, breathing, thinking being. Amazingly, we all have these parts in common, and yet we are all individuals.

Human anatomy is the study of the structure of the body and how the various parts work. This includes bones and muscles, the stomach and nerves, the heart and the brain, and how it all changes as we age. Throughout this chapter, take a close look at yourself as we explore the fascinating body that makes you YOU.

The spectacular human skeleton gives us shape and structure.
It protects our delicate organs, such as the heart and brain.
Our bones also make blood cells and even help us hear!

STRUCTURING YOU

The human body has many
delicate parts inside, such as
the brain, heart, and lungs. The
skeleton is what protects all
of these. The human skeleton is
made up of more than 200 bones,
some quite big and some very
small. Each hand has 27 bones
while each foot is made up of
26. The **skull** protects the brain,
and the **ribcage** surrounds the
heart and lungs. Our skeleton also
provides the body with support,
helping us stand up straight.

OUT OF CURIOSITY

**The smallest bone in the body, the stapes, is
inside the ear. It is just 3 mm (0.12 in) long.
The stapes helps carry sounds to the inner ear.**

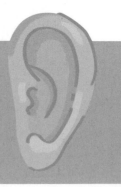

BONES

Connecting bones are muscles and joints that help the body move. Bones contain lots of calcium and other minerals, which make them strong. They can even repair themselves if they get broken. Bones are **living tissues** that grow as we do. Tissues are collections of similar cells, which are the body's smallest building blocks. In this case, bones are made of tiny bone cells.

IN THE BONE FACTORY

Bones have a protective layer of hard, tightly packed bone on the outside. Inside, there is a sponge-like structure that makes them light. Bones are slightly flexible, but become more rigid as you age. Inside many bones is **bone marrow**, where blood cells (see page 96) are made, around 500 billion of them every day.

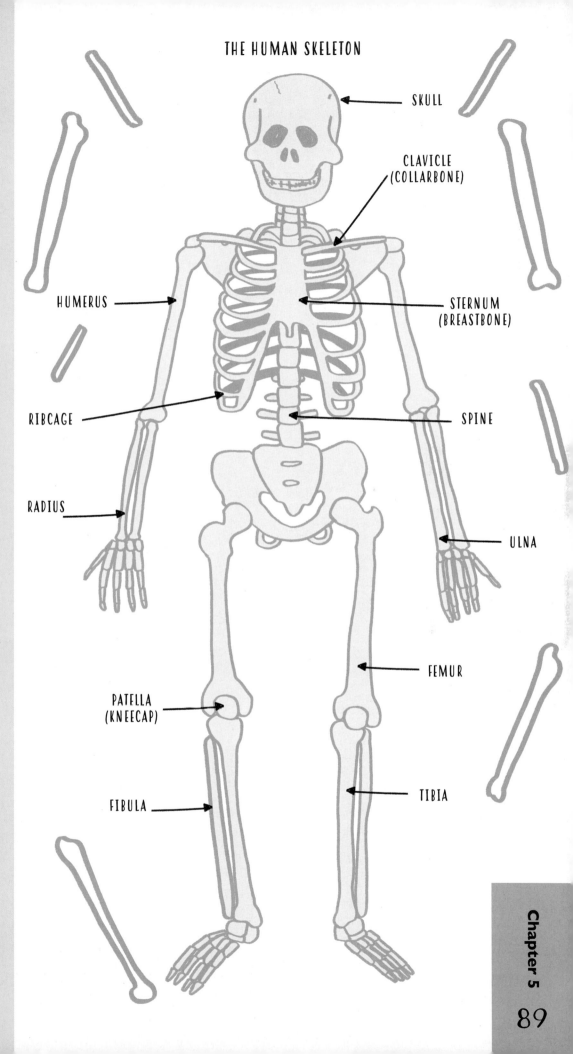

THE HUMAN SKELETON

SKULL

CLAVICLE (COLLARBONE)

HUMERUS

STERNUM (BREASTBONE)

RIBCAGE

SPINE

RADIUS

ULNA

FEMUR

PATELLA (KNEECAP)

FIBULA

TIBIA

MOVING AND GROOVING

The skeleton holds up the body, but how do the hundreds of bones work together to allow us to walk, run, grip, and stretch? That's where muscles and joints come in. Without them, we would be just a pile of bones!

JOINTS

Some bones are joined firmly together, such as in the skull. Others are connected with joints. **Synovial joints** connect bones that give us a large range of motion, such as in our arms and legs. They ensure that the ends of bones don't rub against each other and wear down when moving. Inside these joints, several parts work together. At the end of the bone is a smooth **tissue** called **cartilage**. It sits in a slippery liquid called **synovial fluid**. A **ligament** connects the bones in the joint to keep it all together.

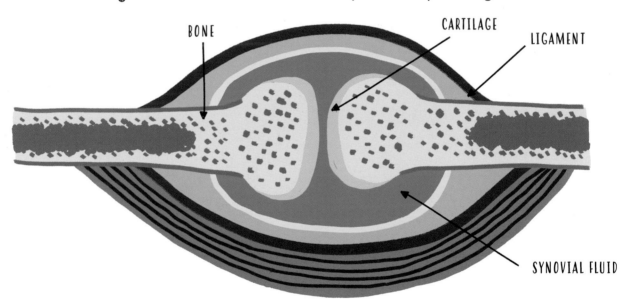

BONE

CARTILAGE

LIGAMENT

SYNOVIAL FLUID

MUSCLES

To be able to move, bones and joints also need **muscles**. These are like stretchy cords that attach to bones using **tendons**.

Muscles work by **contracting**. This means that they shorten and tighten, pulling on the bone as they do so. If the bone has a joint, it can then move. But muscles can only **pull**. If they pull an arm up, the same muscle is unable to push it down again. The clever human body solves this problem by having each muscle work with another, in groups of two called **antagonistic muscles**. Each muscle is part of a pair that works in two directions.

For example, to bend the elbow, the arm has both a **biceps** on the front of the arm and a **triceps** on the back. Each one can contract to pull the arm up or down. To pull the arm up, the biceps contracts while the triceps relaxes. Then, to push the arm down again, the biceps relaxes while the triceps contracts.

CONTRACT AND RELAX

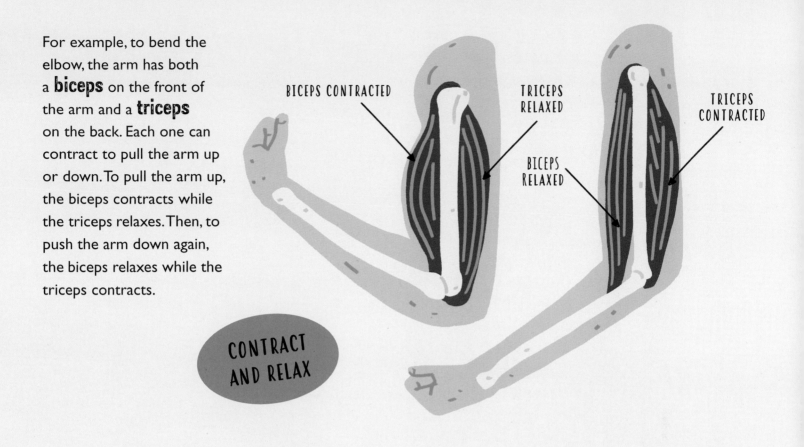

BICEPS CONTRACTED

TRICEPS RELAXED

BICEPS RELAXED

TRICEPS CONTRACTED

WORKING TOGETHER

Many muscles work together when your body wants to move. Your body has more than 600 of them, after all! Wiggling your fingers takes several muscles at once. A runner needs to use both arm and leg muscles to pump their arms while they bend their legs and run. If you're dancing, you might use pairs of muscles all over to really groove with your whole body. Even a smile uses at least ten muscles to move your mouth.

Even while you're sleeping, the organs in your body are working hard. They have many different functions but one thing in common. They all help you live!

ORGANS

An organ is a group of tissues that work together to do a specific and important job. These are some of the main organs in the human body.

Lungs: When you breathe in, air travels down to the lungs. They take the oxygen from the air and put it in your bloodstream. They also remove carbon dioxide from your blood and breathe it out.

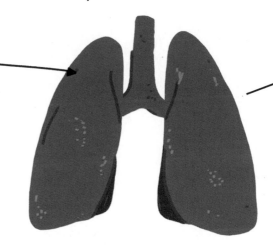

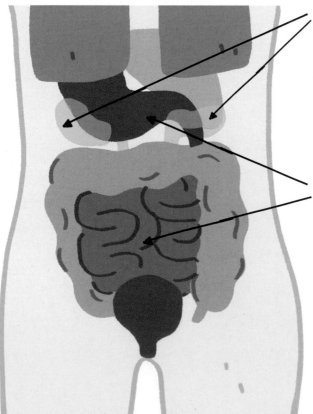

Kidneys: The two bean-shaped kidneys work as a filter for the blood. They clean out waste and extra water, to keep the body perfectly balanced. The waste is sent on to the bladder and leaves the body as urine.

Stomach and intestines: These organs are part of the **digestive system**. The stomach breaks down food into mush. The food then travels through the intestines, which absorb the water and nutrients.

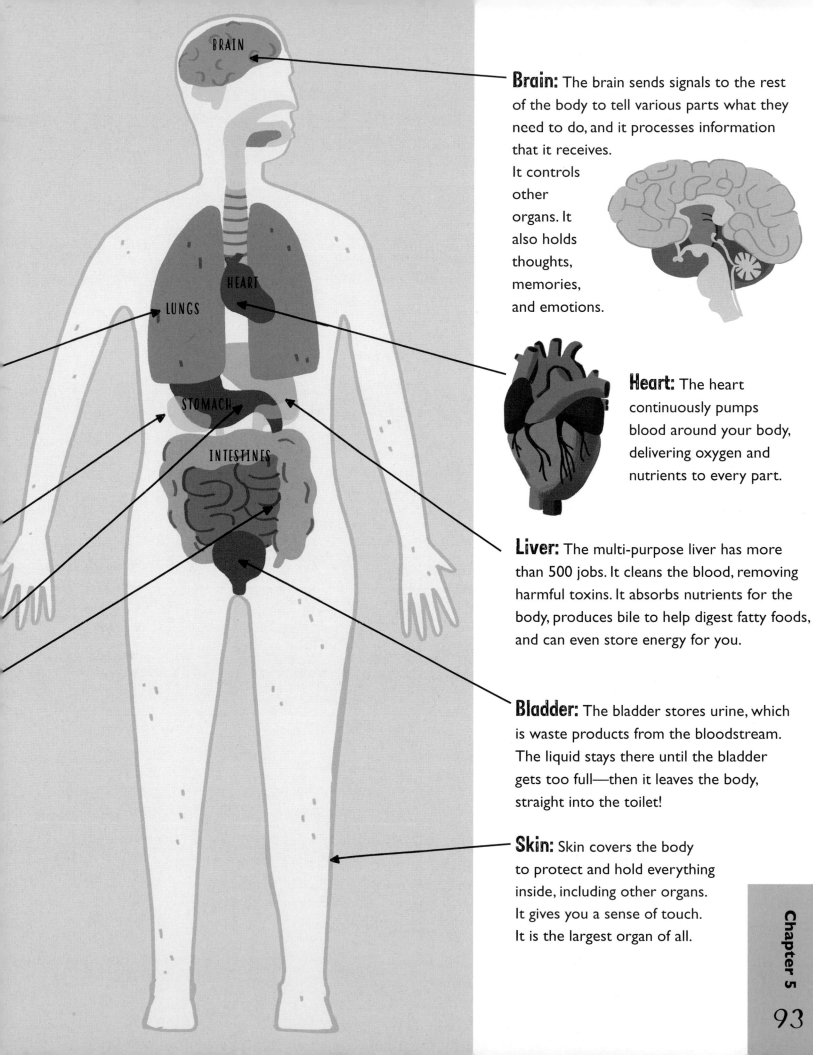

Brain: The brain sends signals to the rest of the body to tell various parts what they need to do, and it processes information that it receives. It controls other organs. It also holds thoughts, memories, and emotions.

Heart: The heart continuously pumps blood around your body, delivering oxygen and nutrients to every part.

Liver: The multi-purpose liver has more than 500 jobs. It cleans the blood, removing harmful toxins. It absorbs nutrients for the body, produces bile to help digest fatty foods, and can even store energy for you.

Bladder: The bladder stores urine, which is waste products from the bloodstream. The liquid stays there until the bladder gets too full—then it leaves the body, straight into the toilet!

Skin: Skin covers the body to protect and hold everything inside, including other organs. It gives you a sense of touch. It is the largest organ of all.

Labels on diagram: BRAIN, LUNGS, HEART, STOMACH, INTESTINES

BRAIN CONTROL

While some animals, such as slugs, can live without a brain, humans wouldn't be who they are if they didn't have one. The brain helps us move, think, feel, talk, remember, and so much more.

WHAT DO YOU THINK?

The brain is a complex and busy organ. It is made up of billions of brain cells and uses 20% of the body's energy to keep us going. It is in charge of many different functions. Some of these help the body work, such as keeping your heart beating or your muscles moving, while others control your thoughts, emotions, and senses. Different parts of the brain help control different functions.

CEREBRUM

HYPOTHALAMUS

CEREBELLUM

BRAINSTEM

BRAIN POWER!

Cerebrum: The largest part of the brain is the cerebrum. It is the outer portion of the brain, with a deeply folded surface. This is where complex thinking and understanding happen. The cerebrum controls your personality and speech, processes sight and touch, helps you make sense of emotions and the space around you, and directs the rest of your brain and body when you decide to move.

Cerebellum: The cerebellum sits at the back of the skull. It helps control your muscles and movement, by assisting with balance and coordinating your body so you move smoothly.

Brainstem: At the bottom of the brain and the top of the spinal cord is the brainstem. It helps with the things that you don't normally "think" about to make your body work, such as keeping your heart beating and your lungs breathing.

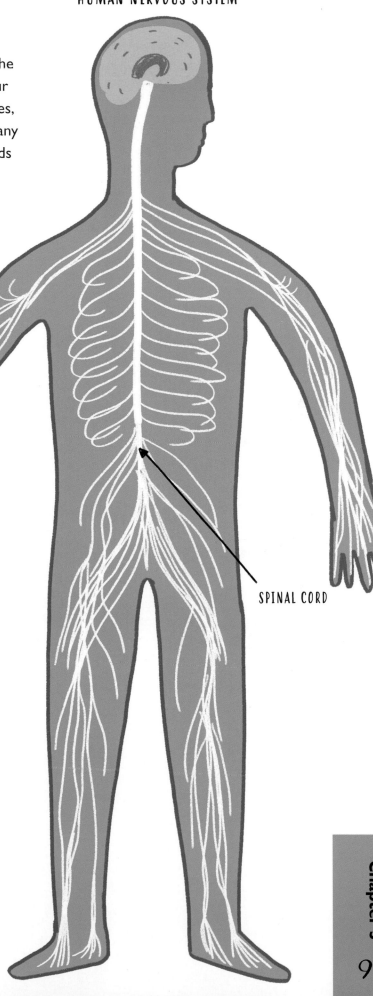

HUMAN NERVOUS SYSTEM

SPINAL CORD

Hypothalamus: The hypothalamus may be only the size of a pea, but it plays a big part in regulating your body. The hypothalamus regulates a lot of hormones, which are the chemical messengers that control many aspects of how the body works, grows, and responds (including sleep, thirst, and hunger).

LEFT AND RIGHT

The brain is split into two sides, or **hemispheres**. The **left side** controls the actions of the right side of the body. The **right side** of the brain controls the left side of the body.

NERVOUS SYSTEM

The brain is part of the body's **nervous system**. This system also includes nerves and the spinal cord. The spinal cord is a nerve "highway," a key part of the network of nerves all through the body that carries signals and messages to and from the brain. The spinal cord can even handle some nerve messages itself, without sending them to the brain. The instinct that makes you move your hand away from a flame is triggered just by the spinal cord so it can be started super quickly.

Blood flows through the body in blood vessels, transporting vital materials and waste. From the powerful beating heart to tiny capillaries, each element works together as part of the circulatory system.

CIRCULATORY SYSTEM

The job of the **circulatory system**, or **cardiovascular system**, is to take blood around the body, delivering oxygen and nutrients and clearing out waste. It is made up of the heart, blood vessels, and the blood itself.

PUMPING LIFE

ARTERIES

VEINS

BUSY BLOOD

The red substance you might see if you cut yourself is a very important delivery system for the body. It transports different types of cells, which each have a particular job. **Red blood cells** bring oxygen to every part of the body and take away carbon dioxide. **White blood cells** fight any intruders that might cause disease. **Blood platelets** help the blood clot, or clump together, to fix cuts and stop blood from leaving the body.

HUMAN CIRCULATORY SYSTEM

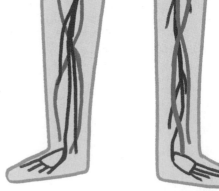

BEATING HEART

The heart is a powerful **muscle**, about the size of your fist. When the right side of the heart contracts, it pumps blood that has returned to the heart from the lungs out into the body. When the left side contracts, it takes blood from the lungs and pumps it to the body. Each **heartbeat** is the muscles contracting. The heart can beat more than 100,000 times in a single day—that's over 35 million times in a year! The average person's heart will beat more than 2.5 billion times in their lifetime.

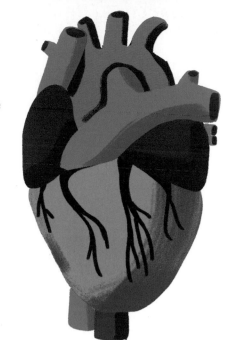

HUMAN HEART

 # BLOOD VESSELS

The blood vessels are like a network of roads that travel all through your body, allowing the blood to travel from one place to another. **Arteries** take blood away from the heart, delivering oxygen and nutrients to the body. **Capillaries** are smaller tubes that branch out and take the blood from the arteries to specific areas. **Veins** then take the blood back to the heart. The blood cycles to the lungs for more oxygen, then repeats the journey again.

 # HEALTHY HEART

The heart works hard day and night, always pumping to keep you alive. If you use up more oxygen than usual, such as when you exercise and are breathing harder, the heart needs to pump even harder to keep up. A healthy heart will eventually return to its normal rate of beating after the exercise stops.

STAGES OF FOOD

The food on our plate is delicious to eat. It looks and tastes good. But as it is, it can't actually DO anything for the body. It needs to be broken down into simper materials to be of use.

 ## DIGESTIVE SYSTEM

Digestion means breaking down food into substances that the body can absorb and use. The **digestive system** is the group of organs that process food through all stages. The **digestive tract** travels all the way from your mouth to your bottom!

 ## TAKE A BITE

The first step in a food's journey is when it enters the **mouth**. The teeth chew it into pieces small enough to be swallowed. It is then pushed into a **muscular tube**, the food pipe, which squeezes it down to the **stomach**.

 ## BREAKING DOWN

Food sits in the **stomach** for several hours, while powerful muscles and juices break it down into smaller pieces yet again. This slushy substance then travels into the **small intestine**, where many of the nutrients are absorbed into the bloodstream.

MOUTH

FOOD PIPE

SMALL INTESTINE

HELPERS

An **acid** in the stomach helps break down food and get rid of anything harmful. In the small intestine, **bile** (a liquid produced by the liver) helps break down fat. To break down food really well, the organs also have help from **enzymes**. These are proteins made by the body that speed up chemical reactions. In a chemical reaction, two or more materials react with each other, forming new materials. In the mouth, enzyme-carrying **saliva** starts the digestive process as it mixes with food.

OUT OF CURIOSITY

In your lifetime, your body produces enough saliva to fill two whole swimming pools!

STOMACH

LARGE INTESTINE

RECTUM

ANUS

IRRITATION

If the body is unable to break down a certain type of food, the person suffers a **food intolerance**. For example, people who are **lactose intolerant** are usually missing an enzyme that can digest the sugar called lactose in milk products. Some chemicals added to food can also irritate a person's digestive system.

MOVING OUT

Finally, the mush moves on to the **large intestine**. Water and remaining nutrients are absorbed, leaving anything else to dry out. This waste then moves to the **rectum** where it is stored as poop. Eventually, it is pushed out of the body through the **anus**.

Making sense of our surroundings begins with the sense organs. Special receptors around your body take in information from the world and pass it to your brain. Your brain carries out the process of making sense of your surroundings so that you can live safely and happily.

SENSES

Your body has many special **receptors** that can sense the world. They take in information about what is sweet, soft, hot, and more, and send it to the brain to process. There are five main **senses**—sight, smell, taste, touch, and hearing.

 ## SIGHT

Your **eyes** sense shades, shapes, brightness, and distance. Light reflects off objects, then enters through the central black **pupil** and passes through a **lens** to the back of the eye. Millions of receptors gather information about brightness and color, then send it on to the brain through the **optic nerve**. The brain can then put together an image and understand the object that you see before you.

 ## SMELL

When we breathe in through the **nose**, smells (which are chemicals) enter the body. Slimy **mucus** traps the chemicals at the back of the nose, where receptors send signals to the brain. The brain can then figure out what the smell is. Humans are able to make out about 10,000 different smells.

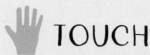 # TOUCH

Covering the whole body, our **skin** plays a huge part in sensing the world. Just under the surface, receptors sense pressure, heat, cold, and pain. They send signals through the nervous system to help the body react to the touch. If the body feels cold, for example, its little hairs will react by standing on end to trap warm air. The feet contain more sense receptors than most parts of the body. This is why they are so ticklish! They might react by kicking, without you even thinking about it.

TASTE

Your **tongue** is covered in thousands of tiny **taste buds** to help you taste the food you eat. Each taste bud is a sense receptor that sends a signal to the brain about the food—whether it's sweet, salty, bitter, sour, or umami (tasting rich, like meat or mushrooms). The brain puts all the signals together to understand the taste of the meal. The sense of smell works very closely with taste to give a full understanding of food. These senses help you enjoy a delicious dish, but they can also warn the brain if a food is unsafe to eat!

HEARING

Sounds enter the body through the **ears**. Sound waves (vibrations that travel through air or water) travel through the ear canal to the ear drum. This vibrates when it feels sound waves—the louder the sound, the bigger the vibration! The vibrations move on to hearing receptors that turn them into signals for the brain. The brain makes sense of them.

AND MORE

Proprioception is often described as the sixth sense. It makes use of receptors in muscles and joints to help you understand your body's position in space. Without it, you would fall over all the time!

THE CHANGING HUMAN BODY

Just like any other life form, the human body changes over time.
It is born, grows bigger, and gets older—with lots of excitement along the way!

BABY

When cells from a mother and a father join inside the mother, a baby's journey begins. It stays inside the mother's **womb** for nine months, growing and developing until it is ready to enter the world. Once born, it is small and depends on its parents for food, getting around, and safety. The baby very quickly grows and learns, soon recognizing faces and exploring its surroundings with its hands, mouth—and all its senses.

CHILD

Learning continues at a speedy rate as children learn to walk and to talk. Language grows as children hear words repeated, then begin to connect them to their meanings—and finally to use them! Twenty baby teeth start forming before a child is born, but they move down from the gums between the ages of 6 months and 12 years. Between age 6 and adulthood, baby teeth fall out as the 32 larger, permanent teeth move into place.

ADOLESCENT

Between the ages of 8 and 14, girls start going through **puberty**. Boys start a little later, between 9 and 16. During puberty, the body changes so that—when its owner is old enough—it would be able to make a baby, if they wanted! **Adolescents** have a growth spurt, when they grow taller quite fast. They grow hair in new places, start to sweat more, and may develop acne. Girls develop breasts, and boys' voices become deeper.

ADULT

Around age 21, a human has usually reached their full height and may have their complete set of **adult** teeth. Adults may choose to start a family. When a woman has a baby in her womb, she is said to be **pregnant**.

OLD AGE

After many years of adulthood, a person begins to approach **old age**. Their skin becomes less firm, causing wrinkles, and their hair may turn white or start to fall out. Their cells are less able to repair themselves or make good-quality copies of themselves. Some organs and systems of the body start to work less well.

OUT OF CURIOSITY

There are around 8 billion people living across the world. The average age of all those human beings is 29.

Your body is the most important thing you have. It works hard for you, so, in return, you must take good care of it to keep it going strong for years to come.

HEALTHY EATING

The food you eat can be good or bad for your body. Humans must eat a balanced diet to stay healthy. This means choosing a variety of foods.

Carbohydrates, found in bread and pasta, and **lipids** (fats and oils), found in food such as butter and fish, give you energy. **Proteins**, found in meat, fish, nuts, and eggs, can help make new cells or repair muscles. **Vitamins** and **minerals** are found in foods including fruits and vegetables. They keep you healthy and strong.

IN MODERATION

It is important to eat these nutrients in the right amounts. Too much of some of them can make you sick. Eating too many fatty foods causes **obesity**. This means there is more fat than your body needs, and it puts extra pressure on your body to do its work—the heart and lungs need to work harder, for example. Not eating enough vitamins and minerals can weaken your body and make it harder for it to perform everyday processes. It is important to eat several portions of fruit and vegetables every single day. It is also crucial to drink plenty of water, which is needed by every cell in your body.

🍎 KEEPING MOVING

Exercising regularly helps the body in many ways. The more you exercise, the greater your **lung capacity** will be. This means more oxygen can come into the body. Your heart benefits from exercise, as it builds its stamina and improves blood circulation. Exercise also helps build muscles, keeps the brain sharp, and can even increase **happiness**.

🍎 EFFECTS OF SMOKING

Smoking is very bad for your health. Cigarettes contain **harmful** substances such as tar, nicotine, and carbon monoxide. These coat and damage the lungs, making it much more difficult for the lungs to do their job. These substances can also harm your heart. Nicotine increases the heart rate and narrows blood vessels, making it harder for blood and oxygen to pass through. And, nicotine is very **addictive**. Once you start using it, it is very difficult to stop.

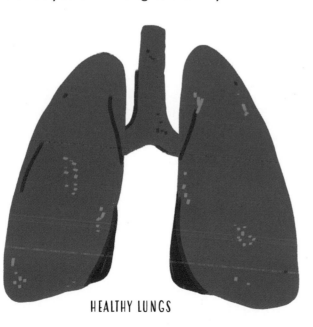

HEALTHY LUNGS

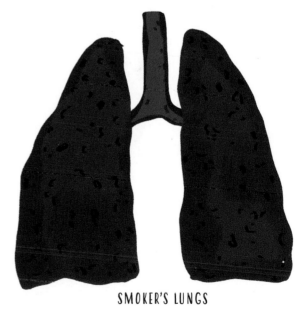

SMOKER'S LUNGS

🍎 DOING HARM

Other substances such as alcohol and illegal drugs have a negative effect on the body. They can **damage** various organs, including the liver, heart, and brain. It is extremely important to be aware that everything you put into your body will affect it. Stay mindful of this, and your body will thank you in the future!

CHAPTER 6

EVOLUTION: FROM PAST TO PRESENT TO FUTURE

In the grand scheme of Earth, humans have been around for only a very short period of time. There is a rich history to be discovered long before our lives here. How did life begin on this planet? How has it changed, or evolved, over time? Where is it going next?

Evolutionary biology is the study of the processes of evolution that have led to the many living organisms found in our world today. Travel through time in this chapter as we explore where it all began, the species that have come and gone, and whether we're alone in this great big Universe.

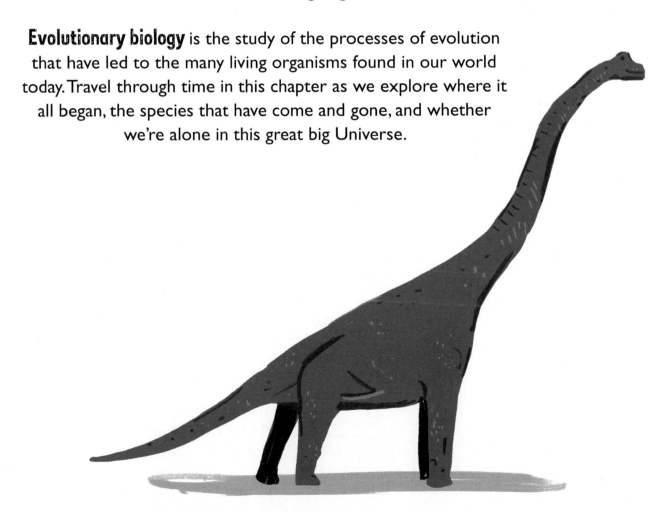

THE EVOLUTION DISCUSSION

By examining fossils from thousands or millions of years ago, scientists can see that species have changed over time. Biologists have worked hard for over a century to understand how and why these changes happen.

 ## CHARLES DARWIN

Evolution is the gradual process of living organisms developing over time on Earth. In 1858, English natural historian and geologist **Charles Darwin** put forward his theory of **natural selection** as the cause of evolution. A year later, he published a book called *On the Origin of Species*, and started the discussion about evolution. His ideas were challenged at the time and have been further developed since, but still underpin current ideas on evolution.

 ## NATURAL SELECTION

Nature is harsh. Animals, plants, and other living things need to compete to survive. Natural selection is the process where the species that are best **adapted** to their environment survive and reproduce, while other species die out. This happens over long periods of time. The better-adapted creatures survive long enough to have babies, passing on their **genes** (the instruction manuals in their cells, giving them sharp teeth or thick fur) to their babies, who carry on the strong line of species, perhaps even adapting to fit the environment even more. In contrast, over time, if less well-adapted animals often die before adulthood, their species will eventually die out.

EYE-OPENING ISLANDS

Charles Darwin spent many years exploring the world and studying hundreds of plant and animal species. When in the **Galápagos Islands** (a group of islands in the Pacific), he noticed some small but important differences among the wildlife. For example, on some islands, some finches had pointy beaks for snapping up insects. Other finches had rounder beaks for cracking seeds. Darwin realized that each species had evolved from one original species of finch, adapting to have characteristics that suited the foods available in their specific home. His theory of natural selection was born.

LIGHTBULB MOMENT!

DARWIN'S FINCHES

CHANGES OVER TIME

Evolution happens over millions of years. As a species adapts, its strongest features are passed on to the next generation. Little by little, these **characteristics** take over and the species changes. Eventually, a new species entirely might evolve! For example, we know what a whale looks like today—large body, huge flippers … But did you know that today's whale evolved from an ancestor that walked on four legs? Around 55 million years ago, an animal called **pakicetus** lived on land but sometimes ate fish. Over millions of years, it evolved to have a stronger tail for steering in water, and its legs turned into flippers!

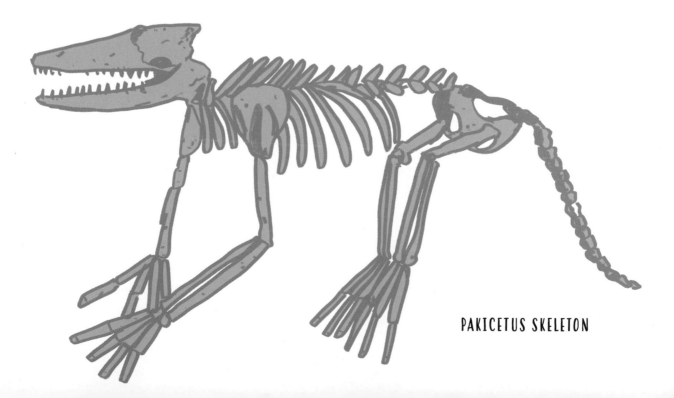

PAKICETUS SKELETON

THROUGH TIME

From tiny organisms to ginormous creatures, planet Earth has seen many things come and go during its time in the Solar System.

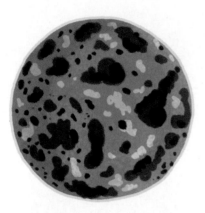

3.8 billion years ago:
The first life appears! These are simple single-celled organisms that live in the oceans. Over millions of years, they start to provide oxygen to the water and atmosphere.

1.5 billion years ago:
More complex cells, with internal structures capable of doing different jobs, start to form in the oceans.

4.5 billion years ago:
Earth forms, but it is nothing like we know today. Its surface is hot, molten rock. It is millions of years before Earth cools and rain begins to create oceans.

395 million years ago:
The first four-legged animals appear. They are amphibians, able to move between water and land.

312 million years ago:
Reptiles evolve from amphibians. Around 80 million years later, a group of reptiles called dinosaurs has evolved.

150 million years ago:
Birds have evolved from a group of small, feathered dinosaurs. Birds are the only "dinosaurs" alive today.

665 billion years ago:
The first animals, which are simple invertebrates (without a backbone), evolve in the ocean.

520 million years ago: Vertebrates (with backbones) emerge. They are simple, jawless fish.

1 billion years ago:
Living things made of more than one cell appear.

540 million years ago:
Some invertebrates start to grow shells.

OUT OF CURIOSITY

If you shrunk the history of Earth down to a 24-hour period, humans would only appear in approximately the last minute! So much has gone on before us.

65 million years ago:
The dinosaurs are wiped out after the impact of a giant space rock. Over millions of year, mammals grow larger.

350,000 years ago:
Modern humans have evolved. We are descendants of great apes that lived 4–7 million years ago.

Chapter 6

111

CLUES TO THE PAST

Humans have only been on this planet for a very short time. So how do we know what happened before us? Luckily, the Earth and its many inhabitants have left clues that give scientists a picture of how our world looked in the past.

PLANT FOSSIL

PERFECT PRESERVATION

When a living organism dies, it usually rots and is destroyed over time. But sometimes, its remains happen to be preserved in the ground. These remains or imprints of prehistoric organisms are called **fossils**. Over millions of years, the remains harden, while the surrounding mud or sand turns to rock. Some fossils have also been found trapped in amber resin, tar, or ice. The oldest fossils found date back to **3.45 billion years ago**.

FOSSILS SPEAK

Extinct animals can speak to us through the fossils they left behind. For example, footprints and dinosaur bones can reveal the size of these mysterious animals and even explain what they ate and how they moved. By looking at fossils through time, we can also see how creatures have evolved. Though **trilobites** became extinct millions of years ago, these small shelled animals survived in the oceans for almost 300 million years. Studying trilobite fossils shows scientists how they changed over their time on Earth. Studying the different plant fossils found in an area can even show scientists what Earth looked like in the past.

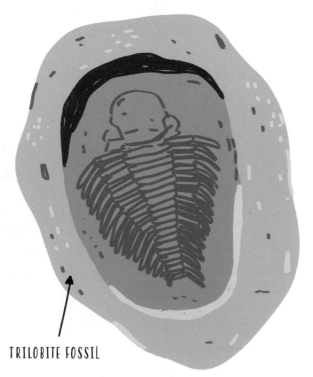

TRILOBITE FOSSIL

FINDING FOSSILS

Many fossils are found by people walking past rock that has been exposed, or by those digging up land. In North America, *Tyrannosaurus rex* bones have been found by farmers going about their daily business! **Paleontologists** study fossilized animals and plants. They uncover details about the past, and study them to try and understand what may have happened and why.

WHAT A FIND!

PALEONTOLOGIST

MARY ANNING

Mary Anning was born to a poor family in 1799. She lived by what is now known as the Jurassic Coast, in southern England. From a young age, she spent her time finding and painstakingly digging out fossils. She was the first to discover the marine reptile *Ichthyosaurus*, the first complete skeleton of a *Plesiosaurus*, and even a winged pterosaur. In her time, she gained little credit for her work, because she was a woman. Today, though, she is known to have hugely contributed to science. She even started the study of **coprolites**.

OUT OF CURIOSITY

We often think of fossils as being the bodies of plants and animals. But animal traces such as footprints, burrows, and even poop can be found millions of years later. Fossilized poop is called coprolite.

Evolution is possible because characteristics are passed from parent organisms
to their babies. In organisms that reproduce asexually (make copies of a single parent),
change only happens when there are mistakes in the copying, called mutations.
But in organisms with two parents, features can be mixed and matched quickly and easily.

 ## INHERITANCE

When a baby is born, it **inherits** its features from its parents. This includes characteristics
such as eye shade, hair type, and height. Because babies form from cells from both parents, they
have a mix of features—some from the mother, and some from the father.

CHILDREN WITH FEATURES FROM BOTH PARENTS

Chapter 6

114

VARIATION

All living things pass on characteristics to their offspring. But not all offspring are alike. **Variation** makes differences between them. You and your siblings each have different combinations of your parents' features. And within the species, you are similar to every other human around the world (two legs, intelligent brain, etc.), but there are differences. Some people have blue eyes, and some have brown. Some people are tall, some are short, and some are somewhere in between.

VARYING TO SURVIVE

Variation means that there is variety in the organisms in a species—they are not all **identical**. It comes about by mixing genes from two parents and by mutation, which sometimes changes a feature of an organism slightly. Sometimes one variant of a feature is more helpful to an organism than another. In a snowy environment, an animal born with lighter fur might survive better as it can hide from predators. It will succeed and reproduce, passing on its genes. Over time, more animals will have lighter fur. Variation helps species adapt, over time, to changes in their environment.

 # VARYING TO EVOLVE

Over time, the variations in each new generation lead to evolution. When a species evolves so much that it has wings rather than arms, feathers rather than scales, and a beak rather than teeth, we can say that it is a different type of animal—a bird rather than a dinosaur! Variation has led to the existence of millions of different species on Earth!

ADAPTING TO THE WORLD

In the competitive world of nature, species must fight to survive.
This isn't always a physical battle—sometimes it's all about
finding a particular habitat where there is less competition for food.

ADAPTATION

Over time, a species becomes more and more suited to its environment. This is called **adaptation**. Living things also adapt to the arrival of other species in their environment, perhaps growing larger or sharper-toothed to fight off bigger predators. Over many generations, animals may move into a less crowded habitat, such as the treetops or underground burrows, to avoid competition. Slowly, species adapt to this environment, evolving wings for flight or large paws for burrowing.

PERFECT FIT

We can see adaptations in every animal if we look closely enough! Over time, polar bears have grown thick fur to adapt to their cold land. Elephants, on the other hand, have finer hair as well as large ears that they can fan to keep cool in the heat of their sunny home. Plants also adapt to their surroundings. A cactus has become well suited to its desert habitat. Its long roots can stretch far to collect water, and its thick stem can hold on to the water for far longer than many other plants.

FENNEC FOX

🌵 A TALE OF THREE FOXES

A fox is a mammal. But there are dozens of different species of foxes, each adapted to their own habitat. A **fennec fox** has a unique look, for example. Its huge ears help it release heat and cool down in its hot desert home. Living in the chilly north, the **Arctic fox** doesn't need this feature. Instead, it has adapted to have fur on its paws to keep them warm and stop them from sliding on the ice. Yet another fox species, the **red fox**, has adapted to be resourceful to find food in human settings, such as farms and cities.

RED FOX

ARCTIC FOX

🌵 ADAPTING TO CHANGE

A species is adapted to survive in its part of the world. But what if that habitat changes? If the polar bear's land heats up, its characteristics are no longer suited to its home and it will struggle to survive. Species need to adapt quickly enough to live in changing homes, or move on to new ones.

HOW TO SURVIVE

All creatures have evolved to have their own special survival strategies. Some fight, some hide, and some have evolved to work together for their greatest chance in the harsh world of nature.

 ## FIGHTING TO SURVIVE

To stay alive, each life form must find energy and the other resources it needs. Survival of a species depends on individual organisms' ability to survive and pass on genes to offspring. Over time, changes in the environment, other stronger species, or a lack of resources might cause a species to disappear. The success of the organisms that have developed the best features and strategies to survive in their world is natural selection. It lies behind all evolution.

 ## BREEDING BABIES

Each individual animal is driven to have babies and pass on its own genes. But it benefits the species if the animals that are best adapted to conditions get to have the most babies, so they can pass on their strong genes. In most species, stronger and healthier animals do get to breed more often. For example, peahens (female peacocks) prefer peacocks who are healthy enough to have many bright eyes on their flashy tail feathers, so peacock tails have grown larger.

PEACOCK

DEFEND YOURSELF

If a creature isn't a fighter—it knows that it won't win a fight against a larger or stronger animal—it will **defend** itself to avoid the fight as much as possible. Some use camouflage to hide from predators, some have huge, hard shells for protection, and others use venom or spikes to scare off attackers. Even plants use these techniques. A cactus, for example, has spiky spines that stop herbivores from eating it.

COOPERATION

Some creatures have discovered that they don't need to compete with every other species. Instead, they can **work together** to help each other survive. For example, sloths and algae have a win-win setup. Algae grows on the fur of the slow-moving sloth, helping camouflage the animal in the trees and providing it with nutrients. In return, the algae get a place to live. Beyond that, a moth lives on the sloth, finding food in the algae. It's a close relationship that works for all involved.

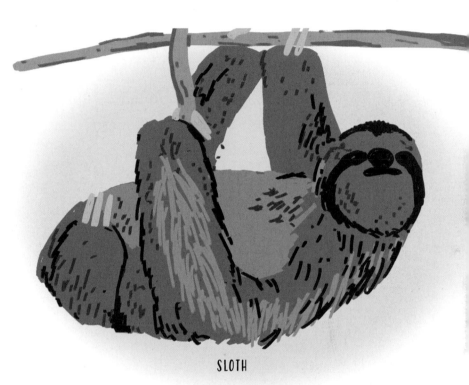

SLOTH

NORWEGIAN LEMMING

MOVING ON

Sometimes, the best way to survive is to move. Some creatures do this regularly, as part of their survival pattern, **migrating** with the seasons, moving to warmer or colder places. Others move only if the environment changes and they need a change to survive. Some Norwegian lemmings will break free from their clan if the space is **overcrowded**. Smaller groups move on to find food in new places.

Chapter 6

119

GOING EXTINCT

Sadly, despite each organism struggling to survive, a species might eventually disappear. Their numbers dwindle in the face of stronger species and changes in the world, which carries on turning without them.

DISAPPEARING ACT

When a species has no more living members, it is **extinct**. This is what happened to the dinosaurs. The **dodo** became extinct in the 17th century. This bird lived on the island of Mauritius, in the Indian Ocean. When humans settled on the island, in 1598, the dodo's forest habitat was soon destroyed. It was a slow bird that did not fly, so it was unable to flee from human hunters and the rats and dogs they brought with them. Within 100 years of its discovery, the entire species had disappeared.

DODO

WHAT HAPPENED

There are many things that can cause a species to go extinct. A major reason is **competition** with another species. If two species are competing for the same food, one can either adapt to find new sources of nutrients, or the weaker species might go extinct. This is natural selection in action. **Changes** to a species' habitat also affect its chance of survival. This could include a new predator moving in, climate change, or a sudden disastrous natural event. Finally, **humans** can have a huge effect on the fate of other species as we take over more and more of the world.

ENDANGERED SPECIES

If a species is at risk of becoming extinct, it is considered endangered. This can happen when its habitat shrinks, for example. When humans clear forests for building or farming, they remove important homes for wildlife. **Orangutans** are critically endangered. They live only on the islands of Borneo and Sumatra in rain forests that are being cut down so the land can be farmed.

ORANGUTAN

GIANT PANDA

ON THE BRINK AND BACK AGAIN

When a species is on the brink of extinction, people such as **conservationists** and scientists often step in. They can help breed more of the species in a controlled space and protect the species' homes. **Giant pandas** have been considered endangered. But thanks to conservation help, their numbers are slowly increasing.

BACK FROM THE DEAD

Just as seeds can be stored to grow plants later down the line, animal DNA can be frozen for future use. This has scientists debating. In theory, extinct species could be brought back to life using their DNA. But should they be?

Chapter 6

121

The world we live in is huge and diverse. There are still areas that remain unexplored, and new species are being discovered all the time.

 ## MILLIONS OF MYSTERIES

Across Earth, around 1.8 million species have been named. But scientists think that there are millions more! Every year, new species are discovered. On top of that, some species are still being classified and named, as scientists work out if they are variations of an existing group, or a new one entirely.

WHAT COULD IT BE?

SURPRISE!

In 2003, the rare **kipunji monkey** was spotted for the first time in Tanzania, Africa. Until then, it was thought to be imaginary. When it was found, it was discovered to be similar to the baboon, but different enough to be its own species. It was like nothing ever seen before! Unfortunately, the kipunji monkey is now listed as **endangered**, and scientists are working hard to protect it.

NEW INFORMATION

With the discovery of new living species comes new **information** about the world we live in. The depths of the ocean have hardly been touched by humans—they are one of the places where few explorers have gone. This means that very little is known about this dark, cold part of the world. People often think that not much survives down there, but recent discoveries might prove otherwise. A number of invertebrates (mostly worms) have been discovered, showing that life has existed there for millions of years, varying into diverse **new species**.

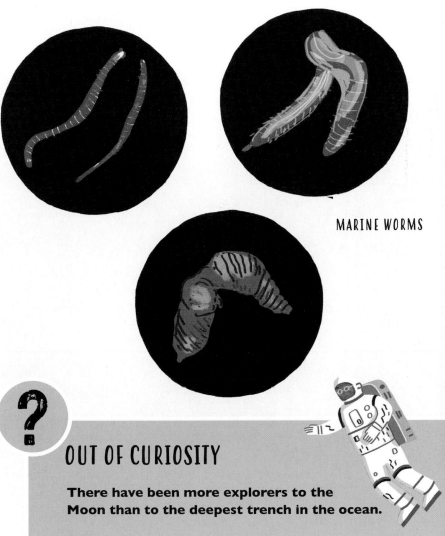

MARINE WORMS

OUT OF CURIOSITY

There have been more explorers to the Moon than to the deepest trench in the ocean.

ACCIDENTAL DISCOVERIES

Thousands of new species are discovered every year. Many of these are in rain forests and oceans, where scientists carefully study and explore the area, but some are found much closer to home—and by **accident**! In 2007, a brand-new species of salamander, called the patch-nosed salamander, was discovered when researchers got lost in Georgia, in the United States. Looking under some leaves by a stream, they found a salamander they could not identify. So, never stop **wondering** at the world around you. You never know what you might find!

LIFE BEYOND EARTH

If there are millions of species on just our one planet,
what might be living out in the great big Universe? This is
something that scientists wonder about and explore every day.

COULD THERE BE?

Planet Earth has developed to offer
the **perfect balance** of sunlight,
oxygen, atmosphere, and nutrients
to sustain life. Not every planet
has these conditions. Some are
too hot or too cold, and some
have other conditions that are
hostile to life. Scientists have
identified about 50 planets
outside our Solar System that
might have the right **conditions**,
but no life has been discovered
yet. That's not to say it won't be
though! Doubtless there are
other planets with the right
conditions for their own life, too,
and we just don't know about them
yet. The Universe is a very big place
with so much still to be discovered.

OUR SOLAR SYSTEM

CLOSE TO HOME

Next to us in the Solar System lies a planet
similar to ours, and yet so different. Scientists
have been focusing on **Mars** to see, first, if there
has ever been microscopic life there and, second,
if anything like life on Earth could survive on this
planet. The planet is colder than ours, with harsh
radiation, but scientists think there might once
have been water there, making it similar to the
early days of Earth. Water could even exist below
the surface—could small bacteria be hiding there,
too? Scientists send robotic rovers to explore
and test the soil for past or current life.

MARS ROVER

☀ LIFE ON THE MOVE

In the early 2000s, scientists began experimenting with growing food away from Earth. On the **International Space Station** they have been growing plants experimentally since 2002 and food crops since 2010. They continue to test watering systems and indoor environments that could make it possible to grow food such as peas, leeks, and tomatoes in the harsh volcanic soil of Mars. If we can produce our own food in space, it means exploration journeys can last longer. Instead of packing food that would eventually run out, we could grow it continuously.

As science progresses, the **possibilities** of creating and discovering life become more and more exciting. What might be discovered in your lifetime?

GLOSSARY

adaptation: The changes a species goes through over time to be better suited to its environment.

anatomy: The branch of science that looks at the structure of a human, animal, or other organism's body.

archaea: A group of microorganisms that have been around for a very long time. Many thrive in hostile conditions.

bacteria: Microscopic single-celled organisms with no nucleus. Some can cause disease, and some can be helpful.

biodiversity: The variety of life, either on the whole planet or in a particular place.

biologist: A person who studies or is an expert in living things.

biome: A large community of life suited to a particular climate and landscape.

botanist: A person who studies or is an expert in plants.

botany: The study of plants.

breed: To mate and produce offspring.

cell: The smallest, basic unit that makes up all living things.

chromosome: A tightly coiled strand of DNA in the nucleus of most eukaryotic cells. Chromosomes carry genes.

classification: The arrangement of organisms into groups based on their similarities.

climate: The usual weather for an area over a long period of time.

deforestation: Cutting down large areas of trees.

digestion: The process of breaking down food into substances the body can use.

DNA (deoxyribonucleic acid): The chemical that stores genetic information in a cell.

ecology: The branch of biology that looks at how organisms relate to each other in their surroundings.

ecosystem: The community of interacting organisms and non-living things in a habitat.

endangered: An endangered species is one that is at risk of going extinct.

endoskeleton: An internal skeleton.

eukaryote: An organism that has cells with a nucleus and other separate structures surrounded by membranes.

evolution: The process of living organisms changing and developing over millions of years on Earth.

exoskeleton: A hard covering that provides a rigid external skeleton.

extinction: The complete destruction of a species, with all organisms of that type dying out.

fertilization: The fusion of male and female cells to produce offspring.

food chain: A series of plants and animals that depend on each other for food.

fossil: The remains or impression of a prehistoric organism, usually preserved in rock

fossil fuel: A fuel, such as coal or gas, made from the remains of organisms that died millions of years ago.

gene: A section of DNA that determines a specific characteristic of an organism.

greenhouse effect: The trapping of the Sun's heat by the atmosphere, which in turn warms the Earth.

habitat: The natural home environment of a plant, animal, or other living thing.

inheritance: The passing on of characteristics to offspring from their parents.

invertebrate: An animal without a backbone.

microbiology: The branch of science that looks at microorganisms.

microorganism: An organism so small that it can only be seen through a microscope, such as a bacterium.

migrate: To move daily or seasonally from one region to another.

natural selection: The process where the species best adapted to their environment survive and reproduce, while other species die out.

nucleus: The central part of a eukaryotic cell, which controls its function and stores its DNA.

nutrient: A substance that provides nourishment to grow and maintain an organism.

organ: A group of tissues that work together to do a specific and important job, such as the heart and brain.

organism: A living thing, including plants, animals, fungi, and single-celled life forms.

photosynthesis: The process of plants using sunlight to create sugars out of water and carbon dioxide.

pollination: The transfer of pollen so that plants can reproduce.

predator: An animal that feeds on other animals.

prey: An animal that is hunted and eaten by other animals.

prokaryote: A microscopic single-celled organism with no distinct nucleus or cell membrane, such as bacteria and archaea.

protein: A type of chemical essential for the growth and repair of a living organism.

renewable energy: Energy from sources that won't run out, such as solar or wind power.

species: A group of similar-looking organisms that can reproduce together.

tissue: A collection of similar cells.

variation: The differences in characteristics between individuals of the same species.

vertebrate: An animal with a backbone.

viruses: An infectious biological agent that needs to take over a living cell to make copies of itself. Viruses can cause disease.

zoology: The study of animals and animal life.

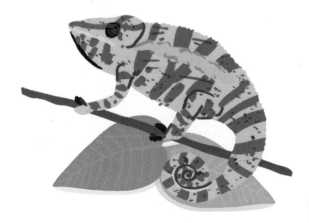

INDEX